Carry on Reading

R

B

By S. A. Stagg and J. A. Wynne
Illustrated by W. M. Ireland

Schofield & Sims Ltd Huddersfield

Foreword

CARRY ON READING is a structured programme, initially in six stages, spanning the reading ages 8 to 12 years. The prime target is literacy through planned reading for interest, information and fun. Each book contains many 'growing points' for conversation, further reading and investigation.

BOOK ONE is for the child with a reading age of about 8 years who has completed a First (or Infant) Reading Course and has acquired at least some of the basic reading skills. There are stories, informative articles, poetry and riddles, covering a wide range of topics, all calculated to appeal to the interests and enthusiasms of children at this stage of development.

At strategic intervals 'Checkpoint' pages appear, which by puzzles and similar devices provide a means of assessing the child's understanding of content and vocabulary in a form which will almost certainly be found entertaining. In this book, the 'Checkpoints' relate mainly to the stories, with the emphasis on vocabulary, and will be found to provide a convenient starting point for additional word study. It is suggested that the informative articles offer a fruitful basis for conversation between child and teacher and, if desired, for further topic study.

The poems and riddle pages add variety and are generally welcomed by the young reader. The verse will provide an opportunity, too, for practice in reading aloud effectively, an art which, regrettably, has been long neglected.

S.A.S.
J.A.W.

First printed 1977
Reprinted 1977 (twice)
Reprinted 1978

0 7217 0294 5
0 7217 0312 7 Net edition

Printed in England by Chorley and Pickersgill Ltd., Leeds

Contents

Acknowledgements

The authors and publishers wish to thank the following for permission to use copyright material:

Evans Brothers Ltd., for the poem FLYING by J. M. Westrup, from *The Book of a Thousand Poems,* published by Evans, London.

Dobson Books Ltd., for the poem SILLY OLD BABOON from *A Book of Milliganimals* by Spike Milligan.

Hodder & Stoughton Children's Books, for an extract from BOBBY BREWSTER'S SHADOW by H. E. Todd.

J. M. Dent & Sons Ltd., for the poem COSY CAT NAP from *The Body Servant* by James Kirkup.

The Gift

One night when the full moon shone clear and bright three friends met in a forest. They were a rabbit, an otter and a crow.

The rabbit gazed up at the moon and said, "The moon is full. We must go to the temple tomorrow with gifts and I have nothing to take."

"Never mind," said the otter, "perhaps I can help you."

Just then the crow, whose ears were keenest, heard something.

"Quiet," he said suddenly, "someone's coming."

The three animals stood as still as statues, looking anxiously to see who else was wandering in the forest in the middle of the night.

Out of the shadows of the trees there came a bent and feeble man, leaning heavily upon a stick. As he drew near he dropped to the ground moaning.

"I'm so tired and hungry," he groaned, "I shall never get out of the forest alive."

"Cheer up, old man!" croaked the crow, hopping on to his chest. "I have some cake in my nest which I was keeping as a gift to the temple tomorrow. You shall have it. I can easily get some more."

And away he flew.

The otter came over and stood near the old man's head. He said, "I, too, was keeping a fish for tomorrow's gift to the temple, but you shall have it. There are many more in the river."

And off he hurried.

The rabbit just stood hanging his head sadly. He had nothing to give and he knew the old man needed much more than a small fish and a piece of cake to keep him alive. What was *really* needed to make him strong again was freshly cooked meat.

The rabbit suddenly had a great thought and danced in the air for joy.

"Old man," he said, "I *do* have something for you, something which will bring back your strength. But *my* gift must be cooked for you. Can you make a fire?"

"Certainly I can," said the old man, "and it will warm my bones, too." Slowly he set to work collecting dry leaves, twigs and sticks. Soon a fine fire was blazing.

When the crow and otter returned with their gifts they were very surprised to see the fire. But they were frozen with horror by what happened next. Their friend the rabbit, after carefully shaking himself from head to toe, leapt straight into the heart of the roaring fire.

Then, to their astonishment, although smoke and flames surrounded him, not a hair on his body was harmed. He seemed to be protected by a great cool green lotus leaf which had appeared from nowhere. More amazing still, the fire went out like a snuffed candle and the old man vanished as if he had never been there at all.

A great quietness settled over the forest and out of the silence there came a gentle voice. It was the voice of the

Overlord of the Spirits and the Destroyer of all Evil. It was the voice of the Spirit of the Temple.

"My friends," said the voice, "I thank you all for your gifts, especially the rabbit. He was not only ready to die in the flames so that I might have cooked meat, but he remembered, before he jumped into the fire, to shake off all the fleas from his body and to save them, too. I therefore order that tonight's noble deed shall be remembered for ever. Look at the Moon."

The voice faded away and a cloud covered the face of the Moon. When it had drifted away the three friends gazed up in wonder. The clear face of the Moon had a strange shadow on it. The shadow was in the shape of a rabbit. And so it has remained ever since.

Checkpoint 

How well did you read?

Who spoke to the old man first?

Why was the rabbit sad?

What surprised the crow and the otter when they returned?

What did the rabbit do before he jumped into the fire?

Why was he not burned?

Whose voice spoke to the three animals?

Make sure of these words

statues surrounded feeble

protected leapt vanished

collecting destroyer

Choose

Each of the words fits one of the pictures, but which?

The Man in the Moon

Do you ever look at the Moon and wonder? For thousands of years people have looked at it and wondered. They have wondered why it was there, what it was made of and whether anyone lived there. They wondered why it sometimes looked like a round bright ball and sometimes like a slice of melon. They have seen the strange marks on it and they have tried to think what the marks were. The marks looked rather like a smiling face to some people, so they began to talk about the *Man in the Moon*.

In many lands all over the world, people made up stories about the Moon and about the man they thought must live there. The stories were all different. The first story in this book, "The Gift", is one. Here is another short one.

An old man and his wife lived in a cottage in the country. The man was a good old man but the old woman was always grumbling at him. She made him do all the work. She was never kind to him and so he was not very happy.

One Saturday night, she found that she had no sticks for lighting the fire next day. She was very cross. She told her husband that he must get up before daybreak the next day and go and gather a bundle of sticks.

"But tomorrow is Sunday," said the old man. "I ought not to go gathering sticks on a Sunday."

The old woman said he must go, so next morning he got out of bed before daybreak when it was still dark. He took his lantern and his little dog and went into the forest not far from his cottage. This forest was called Moon Forest and there he soon gathered enough sticks.

He was about to turn to go home when suddenly the forest was filled with a bright, silvery light. Then the old man was startled by a strange figure standing in the middle of the light. It was the Goddess of the Moon.

The goddess spoke to him. "Don't you know," she said, "that this is my forest? How dare you come here gathering sticks, and on a Sunday, too?"

The old man trembled. He told the goddess that his wife had made him come. She had made him gather the sticks.

He told the goddess how his wife always grumbled at him and how bad-tempered she was.

The goddess listened to him patiently. Then she spoke. "It seems to me," she said, "that your wife is unkind to you. You would be better off on the Moon. I shall send you there."

So the old man was sent up to the Moon. He took his little dog and his lantern and even his bundle of sticks. The people who told this story said that you can still see him there if you look properly.

A good story, perhaps, even if it is not true. But it made people look at the Moon more carefully and soon they began to find out many things about it which *were* true. They saw that each night the Moon moves across the sky. It rises and sets, just like the Sun. They found that it goes round and round the Earth. They noticed that it took about twenty-eight days to go round once. They noticed, too, that only one side of the Moon can be seen; the other side is always turned away from the Earth. Then they found out that the Moon had no light of its own. It only became bright when the Sun shone on it. When the Moon looks round and full, that is because the Sun is shining on all the side we can see. When the Moon is 'new' and looks like a silver bow or a slice of melon, that is because the Sun is only shining on one small part which we can see. All the rest of the Moon is still there, but we cannot see it because it is not lit up. The Moon, in fact, is rather like those 'cat's eyes' in the road which guide motorists at night. They only light up when a light shines on them.

When telescopes were invented much more could be seen. The marks and shapes on the Moon which had looked like a face, or a rabbit, or an old man and his dog gathering sticks, were really shadows made by mountains and valleys. "There is no Man in the Moon, after all," everyone said.

Then, when people knew more about science, they found out even more. The Moon, they discovered, is a very strange place. The days are very hot and the nights are very, very cold. There are no clouds on the Moon and it never rains. There is no water to drink. You cannot fly a kite on the Moon for there is no wind. In fact, there is no air, so you cannot breathe there. People said, "There is no Man in the Moon. No one could live there."

But the age of rockets and spaceships arrived. Russia sent up rockets which landed on the Moon. The rockets had no men in them, but cameras inside took photographs and sent them back by radio. A Russian spaceship, called Luna Three, went round and round the Moon without landing. Its cameras took photographs of the other side of the Moon which cannot be seen from Earth. It is not very different from the side we know. There are mountains and valleys and round holes, called craters, but perhaps it is a little smoother.

Then the first spacemen went to the Moon. There were three of them. They were Americans named Neil Armstrong, Edwin Aldrin and Michael Collins. The spacecraft they went in was called Apollo 11. The rocket was launched in July 1969. Armstrong and Aldrin landed

on the Moon, while Collins circled the Moon waiting to pick them up later. People on Earth watched Armstrong and Aldrin on television as they stepped out of their spacecraft on to the Moon and they could hear what they said by radio.

The spacemen were wearing special clothes which covered them completely. The clothes shielded them from the Sun and, as there is no air on the Moon, they carried their own air supply on their backs.

People on Earth, watching on their television sets, saw the spacemen walking about on the soft dust of the Moon. Their footprints will probably stay there for ever. No rain or wind will disturb them.

The three spacemen returned safely to Earth but on the first night they were on the Moon people looked up and said, "After all, there really is a Man in the Moon tonight."

Checkpoint 

How well did you read?

On which day did the old man gather sticks?
What went with him to the Moon?
How long does the Moon take to journey round the Earth?
Why could you not fly a kite on the Moon?
What was the name of the Russian spaceship which went round the Moon?
What was the American spaceship called which took Armstrong, Aldrin and Collins to the Moon?
Why will the footprints on the Moon last for a long time?

Make sure of these words

different figure cottage telescope
lantern invented launched
journey science exciting

Choose

a word from the list as a title for each of the pictures below. Think carefully, for some words can be used twice, or one picture may have *two* titles.

Flying

I saw the moon,
One windy night
Flying so fast —
All silvery white —
Over the sky
Like a toy balloon
Loose from its string
A runaway moon
The frosty stars
Went racing past,
Chasing her on
Ever so fast.
Then everyone said,
"It's the clouds that fly,
And the stars and moon
Stand still in the sky."
I saw the moon
Sailing away
Like a toy
Balloon.

J. M. Westrup

The Devil in a Nutshell

A boy was strolling along the road eating nuts and making a great deal of noise about it. Suddenly he heard a roaring sound and there before him stood a most frightening gentleman in what seemed to be a red track-suit. He had a long tail, and horns grew out of his head. He was holding a large trident, which is a sort of fork with three prongs. He was also breathing fire and smoke and grinning from ear to ear.

"Hello," said the boy, chewing away vigorously, "who are you?"

"I am the Devil," announced the fiery gentleman, blowing a few smoke rings out of his ears to prove it.

"Is that so?" said the boy, coolly cracking another nut. "I've heard my Mum talk about you. She says you'll get me some day."

"Maybe, maybe," said the Devil. "We must wait and see."

Just then the boy came across a worm-eaten nut. It gave him an idea, for he did not like this grinning, steaming and smoking gentleman much.

"Is it true," asked the boy, "that you can make yourself as small as you wish and even get in a pin-hole?"

"Yes, indeed it is," answered the Devil, moving about a little as the grass where he was standing was beginning to smoulder.

"Could you make yourself small enough to get through the worm-hole in this nut?"

"Of course," replied the Devil. "No problem at all!"

"Let me see you do it then," said the boy.

Promptly the Devil disappeared into the nut. Almost as swiftly the boy stopped up the hole with a piece of twig.

"That's taken care of you!" he muttered and went on his way, whistling and munching nuts which, by the way, is quite a difficult thing to do.

After a time he came to a smithy where the blacksmith was working outside shoeing a horse. Seeing the blacksmith's mighty muscles and his great collection of hammers and pincers, he had another idea.

"Good morning, blacksmith, can you do a small job for me? It won't take a moment."

"Well, I'm very busy," said the blacksmith, wiping the sweat from the end of his nose with a black finger. "What do you want done?"

"It's this nut," said the boy. "I can't crack it." And he held up the nut in which the Devil was trapped.

"That won't take long," said the blacksmith, taking down a small hammer and placing the nut on the anvil.

He gave the nut a light tap and nothing happened. He hit it a little harder. Still nothing happened. He gave it a hearty blow and the hammer handle broke.

"Hmph!" exclaimed the blacksmith. "This is some nut. Where did you get it?"

He took down a larger hammer and tapped the nut again. Nothing happened, but the Devil inside must have been getting anxious. The blacksmith began to get angry with the nut. He glared fiercely at it. He took a personal dislike to it. He seemed to think it was a challenge to his mighty muscles. He had also noticed the boy grinning. So he took down his largest hammer, one which needed great strength to lift, let alone hit anything with.

The blacksmith took several deep breaths, bent his knees once or twice, then lifting the great hammer high above his head he let drive at the nut with all his strength.

There was an explosion like a thunder-clap as the nut flew into pieces. The house shook, the horse bolted down the road, the hammer flew through the air into a field and both blacksmith and boy were tumbled on their backs.

"Cor!" gasped the blacksmith. "The Devil himself must have been in that nut."

"Maybe he was," grinned the boy mischievously.

He dusted himself down and went on his way leaving a very puzzled blacksmith scratching his head in wonder.

What happened to the Devil? Oh, he's around somewhere causing mischief, no doubt . . . or is it only children who cause mischief?

Anyway it's not a bad idea to keep a nut in your pocket. An empty one with a worm-hole in it. You never know, it might come in handy!

Checkpoint

How well did you read?

What was the steaming hot gentleman carrying?
Why did he not remain in one spot for very long?
Where did the blacksmith put the nut?
When he had hit the nut once or twice, how did he feel about it?
What did he do before he hit it with his largest hammer?
Do you think you should *really* keep a nut in your pocket?

Make sure of these words

♠ trident
♥ muscles
♦ mischievously
♣ vigorously
♧ explosion
♢ glared
♡ announced
♠ promptly

Choose

four words from the list as titles for these pictures:

Check

the meanings of these words by matching the signs:

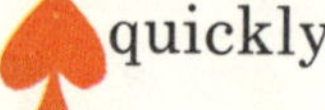 quickly  strongly  biceps  wickedly

The Monster's Riddle

High up on a rock in the land of Greece sat a strange monster. Its body was like a lion's but it had huge wings and its head was rather like the head of a woman. People called it the Sphinx.

Although the busy city of Thebes was not far away, this was a lonely place where few people came, except for one or two passing travellers. For these travellers the Sphinx lay in wait. It would lurk among the rocks until one of them came by and then it leapt out on him. Then it would ask him a riddle, and the only way for the frightened traveller to escape with his life was to answer the riddle correctly. No one ever did.

The riddle was: "What goes on four legs in the morning, two legs in the afternoon and three legs in the evening?" So many travellers were killed that the people of Thebes became frightened and their King worried.

"If anyone can guess the riddle and beat the Sphinx," he announced, "he can have my crown and be King of Thebes, and he can have my sister as his queen as well." As you know, kings in olden days were in the habit of making curious offers like this, particularly if there was not much chance of anyone succeeding.

Time went by and still no one could think of the answer. Then one day a prince came to Thebes. His name sounded

like 'E-D-puss' but was spelled like this: Oedipus. He was a clever fellow and he had made up his mind to find the Sphinx, answer the riddle and get rid of the monster. He set off along the lonely path to the rocks. He was not surprised when the winged lion with a woman's head pounced upon him and asked the riddle.

"What goes on four legs in the morning, two legs in the afternoon and three legs in the evening?" growled the monster. "Think well for your life depends upon it."

But Oedipus was quite calm. He knew the answer.

"Easy," he smiled. "It is a *man*."

"Explain!" ordered the Sphinx.

"Very well," said the prince. "In the morning of his life man is a baby and crawls on all fours, but in the afternoon of his life, when he is grown up, he walks on two legs."

He stopped.

"Come along, come along," roared the monster impatiently. "What about the three legs?"

"Oh, yes," said the prince. "When man is in the evening of his life, when he is old and slow, he walks with a stick. That makes three legs."

There was no doubt that the prince had answered correctly for the monster gave a great cry and rushed off at high speed never to be seen again. Perhaps it only knew one riddle!

Oedipus went back cheerfully to Thebes to claim the reward. (Let's hope the King's sister was not frightfully ugly, and that she liked the look of Oedipus, too!)

This was one of the stories, or legends, told long ago in Greece. In another land, too, called Egypt, they had heard of the Sphinx. They carved a great stone statue of it and placed it in the desert near the Pyramids. It is still there after several thousand years and visitors to Egypt make a point of going to see it. But this Sphinx asks no riddles. In fact, it says nothing at all, although it looks as if it is thinking – maybe of another riddle!

A Page of Riddles

This 'mixed up' picture holds all the answers to the riddles printed below.
See if you can work them out.

What has teeth but never eats?

Old Mother Twitchett had only one eye
And a long tail which she let fly,
And every time she went through a gap
She left a bit of her tail in the trap.

Little Nancy Etticoat
In a white petticoat
And a red nose.
The longer she stands,
The shorter she grows.

What is in church
But not in steeple,
The parson has it
But not the people?

Two legs sat upon three legs
With one leg in his lap;
In comes four legs,
And runs away with one leg;
Up jumps two legs,
Picks up three legs,
Throws it at four legs
And makes him bring back one leg.

The Jackal and the Crocodile

In India the story is told of a little jackal, a kind of wild dog, who long ago lived in the jungle close to a great river. On the muddy banks of this river crawled many crabs and the little jackal was very fond of them. So once a day he paid a visit to the river to catch the crabs and eat them. They were delicious.

In that very same river lived a huge crocodile. He was very fierce and always hungry. He noticed the daily visits of the jackal to catch crabs and thought how nice it would be to have *him* for his dinner.

"I'm sure I should like the taste of that jackal," thought the crocodile, "and I know just how to catch him."

He swam to the edge of the river and kept his head just below the water, with only part of his crusty nose sticking out. It looked just like a little crab.

At dinner time the jackal came trotting along by the side of the river, hoping he would find a crab or two. He saw what he thought was a crab on the surface of the water.

"This is my lucky day," he chuckled. "A tasty little crab! I will scoop it out for my dinner."

He put his paw into the water to scoop it out, but as soon as he did so the crocodile made a grab and his jagged teeth closed over the paw and held it tightly.

The jackal went stiff with fright. He knew that in a moment the great crocodile would drag him into the river and eat him. He had to do something quickly. He called out to the crocodile, as gaily as he could, and said, "Hello, crocodile! Why are you biting my stick? I only put it into the water to scratch your nose for you."

Now although the crocodile was huge and fierce, he was a slow thinker. He believed what the jackal said.

"That's funny," he thought, "I felt sure it was the jackal's paw I grabbed. If it's only his stick there's no use holding on to that." So he opened his mouth and let go.

Quickly the jackal snatched his paw out of the water. Then he laughed.

"Silly old crocodile," he cried, "it wasn't a stick at all. It was my paw and now you've let me go. You are not clever enough to catch me. You are thick in the head."

He ran off into the jungle. The crocodile was furious because he had been tricked and laughed at.

"You may have got away this time, Jackal," he grated, "but you won't do it again. Next time I catch you I shall not let you go."

So he kept hiding in the water with his nose sticking out hoping the jackal would come again. Of course, the jackal was not as stupid as that. He kept well away from the river. But without his crabs he soon grew hungry, so he searched the jungle till he found a wild fig tree. Each day he went to the tree and fed on juicy figs.

After a while the crocodile got tired of waiting about in the river and decided to go and look for the jackal. By good luck, he came across the very fig tree the jackal visited each day. There were signs of the untidy jackal everywhere. So the crocodile gathered a large pile of figs and hid himself underneath them.

At dinner time the jackal came trotting along through the jungle. He was looking forward to a feast of figs, so when he saw the large pile that the crocodile had gathered he was delighted.

"Another lucky day!" he exclaimed. "A fine pile of figs all ready for me. I shall not even have the trouble of picking them."

He was just about to go up to the figs and begin eating when he stopped.

"That really is a strange shape for a pile of figs," he thought. "It almost looks as though something is hiding underneath them."

So, keeping well away from the pile, he called out in a loud voice, "Very odd! Very odd indeed! Usually when I come to the fig tree all the figs in the pile blow about in the wind, because they are so light and tasty. Today they are lying so still that I think they have all gone bad. Perhaps I had better find another fig tree."

The stupid crocodile heard this and thought, "Just my luck! This is a fussy jackal. I suppose I had better move about a bit so that it looks as if the figs are light and blowing in the wind."

So he gave a wriggle or two and, of course, the figs fell off and showed his crusty back.

"You crazy old crocodile," laughed the jackal, as he ran off into the jungle. "If you had kept still I should not have known you were there."

This time the crocodile was even more furious and he hid in some bushes near the fig tree, hoping that the jackal would come back again. Of course, the jackal was too wise to do that, but without his crabs and his juicy figs, he grew very hungry indeed. All he could find in the jungle were a few berries. He grew quite thin.

But the crocodile did not forget him. One day, while the jackal was out hunting, the crocodile dragged himself through the jungle again and came upon the jackal's

house. It was not very large and he had to squeeze himself through the door, but he managed to crawl under the jackal's bed and hide there.

In the evening the jackal came limping home. He had been looking for food all day, but he had not found much. He was hungry and tired and he wanted to curl up on his bed and sleep. He came to the door of his house and was just going in when he noticed that the sides of the doorway were scraped and broken, as though something very large had pushed its way in.

He suddenly felt frightened. Had the crocodile come to his house? Was he waiting inside to grab him? He did not go in, but stood well away from the house and called out, "Good evening, little house. Is anything wrong today? Each day when I come home you always speak to me and say, 'Come in, all is well', but this evening you do not speak and I feel afraid to come in."

Now this was not really true. The house never spoke to him. It was just a trick to see if anyone was inside. But the stupid crocodile was puzzled. He thought he had better reply to the jackal or he would not come in. He did not know how a house sounded when it spoke, but he changed his voice so that it sounded like the noise of sticks rubbing together. He said, "Come in, all is well."

"Oh dear!" thought the jackal, "it's that crocodile again. Now he is inside my house waiting to eat me. If I do not get rid of him there will be trouble. Whatever shall I do?"

After a moment's thought he spoke to the little house and tried to make his voice sound happy. "Thank you, little house," he said, "I'm glad all is well. I shall come in when I've collected some things together."

The crocodile was delighted when he heard this. "How clever I am," he chuckled. "Now I shall catch that jackal at last. I shall really enjoy having him for supper." He licked his crusty lips and clashed his jagged teeth thinking how delicious the jackal would taste.

But the jackal was busy. Quickly, but very quietly, he gathered a large pile of leaves and sticks against the side of his house. When the pile was big enough, he set light to it and it blazed up with a great roar. The crocodile was terrified. He did not want to be cooked. He shot out of the back door and charged off through the jungle. He never came back again. The fire had frightened him too much.

Now the jackal had nothing to fear. How happy he was! He soon made himself a new house, and ate so much that he became overweight. And that is most unusual for a jackal. They are usually just skin and bone and make poor dinners . . . even for crocodiles.

Checkpoint

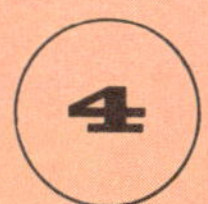

How well did you read?

What was the jackal's favourite food?

What did the jackal say he was trying to do when the crocodile caught him by the paw?

Why did the jackal think there was something wrong with the pile of figs?

What did the jackal eat when he could not get crabs or figs?

What did the crocodile's voice sound like when he spoke from inside the house?

What made the crocodile leave the house in a great hurry?

Make sure of these words

jagged furious juicy chuckled

fierce believed searched delicious

squeeze laughed

Which of the words would you choose as titles for these pictures?

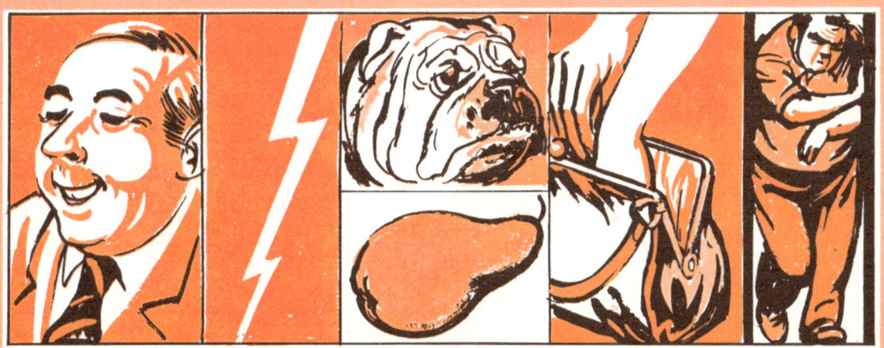

The Tellers of Tall Tales

There once lived in a village in Burma three young men who considered themselves very smart indeed. In fact, they *were* quite quickwitted and so took advantage of many of the simpler people in the village. One way in which they amused themselves was by telling stories about the amazing things they did. Their tales were quite untrue, but they never failed to interest and astound their listeners, so perhaps their mischievous stories were harmless enough. But one day they put their skill at making up stories to a bad use, a kind of stealing. This is what happened.

They were lounging about the village fountain when a

stranger arrived. It was very clear from his beautiful clothes and the jewels he was wearing that he was a wealthy person. The three young men put their heads together and decided how, by using their gift of telling impossible stories, they might get possession of the stranger's fine clothes and splendid jewels.

They waited until the stranger, who seemed a pleasant, friendly man, came over to the fountain.

"Greetings, honourable sir," said the young men in chorus. "Will you not join us at this pleasant spot?"

"With the greatest of pleasure," answered the stranger, a knowing smile lighting up his face. "It will, indeed, be good to have conversation with three fine young men on such a splendid morning."

After a little general talk one of the young men said, "Let each of us tell the story of his most amazing adventure."

"A good idea," joined in the second young man, "but no one may doubt the truth of each story."

"Yes, indeed," added the third young man. "Let us agree that whoever disbelieves the story of another shall give up his clothes and everything he is carrying."

"Agreed, agreed!" said the rich stranger, without so much as raising an eyebrow.

The three young men glanced at each other with knowing winks which said, "We've got a real idiot here. He deserves to lose his possessions." Their idea was, of course, to make their stories so ridiculous that at some point the stranger would say something which would show that he did not believe the story. He would then have to give them his clothes and jewels. What they did not know was that the stranger, quiet, gentle and friendly as he appeared, was an extremely clever person. That was probably why he was rich.

They called the head-man of the village over to act as judge and to see that the bargain was carried out. Soon they were settling down to listen to the first young man's story.

"It is rather odd," he began, "that I am here today at all, for when I was a mere baby somehow I managed to climb a tangerine tree. I sat up there in the branches stuffing myself with tangerines and then, propping myself up in the fork of two branches, I dropped off to sleep. When I woke up I found I could not climb down. There was nothing for it but to go back to the village for a ladder. Luckily I found one, otherwise I might still be up in that tangerine tree."

When the young man stopped speaking, the stranger nodded his head in approval.

The second young man was rather taken aback by this, but he launched into his story.

"My story is about something which happened to me when I was very young, too," he began. "I was playing in the forest when I saw a rabbit scamper into the undergrowth. On tip-toe I went to look for him. Suddenly I found myself facing not a rabbit but a great snarling tiger, his mouth wide open, his teeth gleaming and his body tense and ready to spring.

"'I beg your pardon' I said to the tiger.'I am so sorry to disturb you. Have you seen a rabbit hereabouts?'

"The tiger, his eyes blazing yellow fire, advanced towards me. As he opened his mouth wider to seize me, I took his upper jaw in my left hand and his lower jaw in my right, blew hard down his throat and let go. The tiger gave a great gulp, then turned round and fled. I had been eating onions, you see."

He stopped speaking and looked at the rich stranger who merely nodded his head approvingly and turned expectantly to the third young man.

The third young man had never thought that the game would get as far as this and, like the tiger, gulped then started his story.

"Last year," he said, "I was out in my boat fishing. But

it was a bad day for fishing. After waiting a couple of hours without seeing the slightest sign of a fish I decided to go and find out what had happened to them. So I dived over the side and swam down to the bottom of the river. I soon saw why there were no small fish about, because there at the bottom was a great pike. Quick as a flash, I killed it and then lit a good fire on the bed of the river and cooked some pike cutlets. Then I returned to my boat."

The stranger had not raised even one eyebrow and looked as if he believed every word of this ridiculous story. "Now it's my turn," he said.

"I am the owner of an orange farm. Some months ago something strange happened to one of my trees. It grew larger than any of the others, turned an odd colour and lost all its leaves. But three oranges began to grow. They grew at an unbelievable speed to a stupendous size, then they burst. Out stepped three young men."

"Now," said the rich stranger thoughtfully, "the

orange tree belonged to me so its fruits belonged to me also. Therefore the three young men belonged to me, too, so I set them to work. But they turned out to be lazy rascals and one day they disappeared. I resolved to find these lazy louts, and arranged for my farm to be looked after while I went to search for them."

The stranger stopped and gazed thoughtfully at the three young men.

"Yes," he smiled, "you know very well that you are the three young men and that you are my property. I order you to come back to the farm."

"What?" cried the young men together. "We don't belong to you. We did not grow on orange trees."

A very broad smile indeed spread across the stranger's face.

"Then you disbelieve my story?" he asked cheerfully.

The three young men were filled with alarm. They realised that they had been tricked by the stranger's cleverness. They had lost, for if they said they believed the story they would have to go with the stranger and *work*.

"I claim all your possessions," said the stranger, holding out his hands.

The village head-man nodded in agreement. The three not-so-smart young men had to obey and hand over everything they had there and then. Soon they were walking home shivering and looking very stupid without a stitch of clothing.

They never told any tall tales again.

Checkpoint

Half the words on this page are in the story. Find their partners by checking the signs.

quickwitted decided took advantage
huge silly get possession
astound started mischievous lounging
a small orange from Tangier naughty
tangerine lazing launched clever
ridiculous won unfairly surprise
stupendous take resolved

Here are four sentences. Parts of each sentence have been underlined, and pictures drawn for these parts. Are they suitable?

The three young men put their heads together.

"Greetings, Sire," said the young men in chorus.

. . . . said the stranger, without raising an eyebrow.

The second young man was rather taken aback.

The Speedsters

The strange thing about going fast is that only human beings seem to speed for the fun of it, and they are not really much good at it. In the animal world speed is a much more serious matter. It can mean that the animal either lives or is killed.

The fastest four-legged animal is one of the big cat family, the cheetah. He can reach a speed of 72 kilometres an hour in two seconds, which is a far better performance than most sports cars. The cheetah's top speed is nearly 112 kilometres an hour but, of course, he cannot keep this up for long. Gazelles are probably the champions at travelling fast for a long time, so if they can get a good start they can even escape the cheetah.

The speedsters of the sea have to race in water, and water is about 800 times 'thicker' than air, so their shape is very important. Speedy sea creatures must be streamlined and smooth. Dolphins and porpoises are such creatures. Dolphins have been seen *overtaking* a ship doing 30 knots . . . that's over 50 kilometres an hour.

Sharks and tuna are also speedsters of the sea, but one which may surprise you is the octopus. The octopus, moving about the sea with its tentacles wriggling and grasping, might not be expected to be a speedster, but when danger threatens it becomes jet-propelled. It fills

itself with water and forces it out of a funnel part of its body which can be turned in any direction. A diver has reported seeing an octopus moving so fast that his eyes could hardly keep up with it.

Then there is the squid, which is something like the octopus only it has ten tentacles and an ink bag! This jet-propelled sea creature can squirt out a black cloud from its bag to hide its movements, but sometimes it moves so fast that it shoots right out of the water as high as a house. The record breaker is, however, the sail-fish, a kind of swordfish which is said to reach a speed of about 110 kilometres an hour.

As for birds, two which do not fly, the emu and the ostrich, are very fast indeed. You would never catch them on your bicycle . . . . or a moped either! There is a great

deal of argument about bird speedsters. The humming bird can fly backwards which, perhaps, doesn't count, but diving birds such as hawks and eagles reach speeds of about 170 kilometres an hour. A pilot has reported being overtaken by a falcon when he was diving his aeroplane at 270 kilometres an hour. But the spine-tailed swifts of India are said to reach speeds of nearly 320 kilometres an hour. So *they* must be the champion bird speedsters.

By the way, what about humans on their legs? Walking briskly we get along at about eight kilometres an hour. The fastest runners in the Olympic Games may just reach, for a second or two, a speed of about 37 kilometres an hour. Grandfather could catch them easily on a bicycle! Human beings are not really in the speedster class at all.

Silly Old Baboon

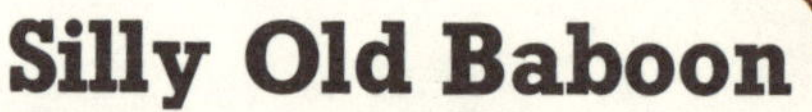

There was a baboon
Who, one afternoon
Said, "I think I will fly to the sun."
So, with two great palms
Strapped to his arms,
He started his take-off run.

Mile after mile
He galloped in style
But never once left the ground.
"You're running too slow,"
Said a passing crow,
"Try reaching the speed of sound."

So he put on a spurt,
Goodness, how it hurt!
The soles of his feet caught fire.
There were great clouds of steam
As he raced through a stream,
But he still didn't get any higher.

Racing on through the night
Both his knees caught alight
And smoke billowed out from his rear.
Quick to his aid
Came a fire brigade
Who chased him for over a year.

If you want to know what happened next you must read the last verse which you will find in a book called 'A Book of Milliganimals' by Spike Milligan.

The Balloon Brothers

In France, about 200 years ago, there were two brothers, one named Joseph, the other Etienne (or Stephen, in English). Joseph was a paper maker whose hobby was inventing things, usually with the help of his brother.

One evening, Joseph was sitting before the fire smoking his pipe and watching the flames go up the chimney. He began to wonder *why* they went up. He thought about it for a while and then got the ladies of the house to make him a small, round, open bag from scraps of silk. He held this near the fire, so that it collected smoke and hot air, and then let go. He watched with great satisfaction as it rose and disappeared up the chimney. The first balloon had been invented!

Joseph talked about his discovery with his brother Stephen and together they made a very large 'balloon' of linen lined with paper. It was open at the bottom. Beneath this they burned a mixture of straw and wool to make what they called 'electric smoke'. The balloon shot up to a height of 300 metres. That is nearly three times as high as the dome on St. Paul's Cathedral in London. This caused a great sensation and they were ordered to give a demonstration before King Louis and his Court.

Joseph and Stephen decided to make a new balloon, big enough to carry three passengers . . . . a sheep, a duck

and a cock. These were placed in a basket which hung below the balloon. When everything was ready the balloon was brought to the Palace yard and the special fire lit. The King and Queen and all the courtiers watched closely until they were driven back by the smoke and the awful smell of burning wool and straw.

Then three cannon shots were fired to signal that the balloon was rising. Today we would say "We have lift-off." Up sailed the balloon with its three dumb passengers. It landed about eight minutes later four kilometres away. It came down with such a bump that the basket burst. The three passengers were scattered unharmed, except for the duck which had its wing trodden on by the sheep. The sheep, being the only one which would never fly on its own, was rewarded by being placed in the comfort of the Royal Zoo for the rest of its life.

This happy success encouraged the brothers to make a balloon large enough to carry human passengers. At first they planned to send up a criminal from prison, who was to be promised freedom if he landed alive. The brothers were not keen to fly themselves. But a man named Rozier said that being the first human to fly was too good for a criminal. He himself would go up in the balloon with a soldier friend.

The great balloon was built with a gallery round the opening at the bottom. The passengers could walk on this and also feed the fire from it. The fire hung in a kind of iron basket in the open neck of the balloon.

So one November day in 1783, watched by a cheering crowd, off went the two men in a balloon. They flew for twenty-five minutes, skimming over rooftops, just missing two windmills and having to rush round the gallery with wet sponges putting out small fires started by the sparks. They landed eight kilometres away.

A balloon craze started. Soon there were all sorts of

balloons floating about the sky, but they nearly all used gas instead of hot air. When aeroplanes were invented, people lost interest in balloons but now, a hundred years later, they are back in favour again. Ballooning has become a sport. The strange thing is that the favourite sports balloon used now is the hot-air type invented by Joseph and Stephen. Instead of burning smelly straw and wool, however, a special gas-torch is used. This is worked by the passengers in a basket slung below the balloon. When they want to go up they turn up the flame and when they want to come down they shut it off. The real trouble with balloons, however, is that you cannot steer them. You just have to drift with the wind.

Checkpoint 

How well did you read?

What was Joseph's work?

How high did the first balloon go?

Why did everyone move away from the balloon when it rose?

What was the signal for 'lift-off'?

How was the sheep rewarded?

Why did ballooning go out of fashion?

Make sure of these words

satisfaction	△	demonstration	⊟
criminal	▽	courtiers	⍋
mixture	⊖	dumb	⌽
sensation	□	scattering	⎅

Choose

meanings for the words by *matching* the signs.

speechless	⌽	throwing anywhere	⎅
no grumbles	△	show	⊟
law-breaker	▽	several things together	⊖
royal folk	⍋	excitement	□

Now cover these and test yourself

The Parachute Men

After the 'Balloon Brothers' adventure, balloons became very popular, especially at fairs. After a time, however, the crowds got bored with watching balloons going up and disappearing out of sight. Sometimes the balloonists tried to make things more interesting by letting off fireworks on the way up. As these quite often made the balloon catch fire, this was rather *too* exciting.

Then there was something new. A man named Blanchard, who had invented a flying bicycle with flapping wings which never managed to get off the ground, had an idea. He dropped things out of the balloon to keep the crowd happy scrambling for little presents. He made an umbrella-shaped bag which slowed down the speed of anything falling through the air. This was the first parachute. The first living creature to fall from the sky by parachute was a cat. So a cat was the first parachutist! Blanchard *said* he made two drops himself, but no one ever saw him do it.

The real father of the parachute was probably another man named Garnerin. In 1797 he built a balloon which carried a parachute and a basket underneath. Garnerin went up to a height of 700 metres and then pulled a cord which released him and the parachute from the balloon. It opened perfectly. This was just as well, for the balloon exploded soon afterwards. Garnerin came down safely, but he was very sick. This was because the air collected by the umbrella shape of the parachute could not escape. The parachute swung violently from side to side, like a ship rolling in a rough sea. Somebody suggested making a hole in the centre of the umbrella shape and this helped steady the parachute. If you have watched parachutes coming down, or seen them on television, you may have noticed that some have curious shapes or open patches. The idea is to stop the swinging movement of the parachute as much as possible.

Parachutes have saved the lives of countless airmen. They are to airmen as lifebelts are to sailors. But great airliners have no parachutes. Perhaps, one day, when an airliner gets into trouble, the pilot will pull a lever and all the passenger part of the airliner will come free and float down gently on a huge parachute.

Garnerin's balloon and parachute adventure of 1797 was repeated in 1960, when the Americans wanted to test the space suit which astronauts would wear when they went to the moon. A brave man named Captain Kittinger went up to a height of nearly 34 kilometres, hanging below a balloon. He was wearing the new space suit. When he jumped he did not open his parachute until he was falling at nearly 1000 kilometres an hour. He tested the suit on the way down. It worked perfectly, and so space exploration and visits to the moon came another step nearer.

Nowadays parachuting, like ballooning, has become a sport for some people. They belong to parachuting clubs. Groups go up in an aeroplane and jump together, but they do not open their parachutes at once. They 'free fall', as they call it. By steering themselves with their arms and legs, they get up to all sorts of tricks on the way down, including releasing coloured smoke from their boots! But, of course, they open their parachutes in time to land safely . . . . at least, most of them do.

The Magic Football Boots

When he was young, the only football Bobby Brewster played was kicking about on the lawn with Mr Henry Brewster — that's his father. They used a tennis ball, with two coats on the ground for goal-posts, so Bobby wore his ordinary shoes for that.

Of course, before he went to Miss Trensham's school, Bobby Brewster had to buy some football boots. He was quite excited when he went to the shop with his mother, and they chose a very smart brown pair with white laces and studs underneath. As a matter of fact, Bobby was so excited that he insisted on walking home in them, but the studs felt so funny on the hard pavement that he never tried that again.

At Miss Trensham's school the boys played football every Monday and Thursday morning. On Bobby Brewster's first Monday morning they stopped lessons at 11 o'clock, and all the boys took their white jerseys and their football boots off their pegs. Miss Trensham was most particular about their appearance and behaviour outside, and she made them all tie their jerseys neatly round their necks by the sleeves and hang their football boots over their right shoulders by the laces. Then off they marched in twos down to the town ground. Miss Trensham stopped the traffic in the High Street, and they really looked a most impressive sight marching over the

crossing. They put on their jerseys and football boots in the pavilion, Miss Trensham led them on to the football field, and the game started.

As a matter of fact, Bobby Brewster was very disappointed with his first game of football. He was one of the smallest boys there, and he found it very difficult to run fast in his new football boots. Once, he even took a huge kick at the ball, missed it and fell down backwards, which made the other boys laugh and Bobby Brewster feel rather silly.

When his mother came to fetch him from the ground, she asked him how he had enjoyed the game.

"Not much," he said.

"Why not?" asked Mrs Brewster.

"Well," said Bobby, "for one thing these football boots are silly. They're much too stiff; I can't run properly in them and, what's worse, when I try to kick the ball they make me miss it."

Mrs Brewster didn't say anything more. She thought to herself that, after all, Bobby Brewster was about the smallest boy in the game, so he couldn't expect to do very well at first. It would have been tactless to say so, though, particularly when he was so disappointed.

When they got home there were a few minutes before dinner time, so Mrs Brewster said she would clean Bobby's football boots before putting them away.

"I shouldn't bother," said Bobby Brewster. "They're silly."

"Never mind. You'll soon get used to them if you look after them properly," said Mrs Brewster. So she cleaned all the mud off and put them into the cupboard under the stairs.

The next Thursday morning, before school, a funny thing happened. When Mrs Brewster gave Bobby his football boots, they were quite muddy. She was rather surprised, but it was time to get off to school, so she didn't say anything. Bobby enjoyed his football better that day. He still wasn't a very good player, but at least he didn't fall down instead of kicking the ball, and once he even managed to kick it twice before any of the other boys could touch it. When he got home after football, he thought he would clean his own boots, and his mother showed him how to do it.

Well, believe it or not, the following Monday morning when Bobby fetched his football boots to take to school, they were muddy again. He knew he had cleaned them after the last game, and he couldn't understand what had happened, but there was no time to ask his mother, so he went off to school and forgot all about it. Football that day was really quite exciting, and Miss Trensham even said "Well played, Brewster!" twice. When Bobby put the boots away that morning, he cleaned them carefully and gave them an extra polish.

Now comes the really funny part of the story. That night when Bobby was asleep, he was wakened up by a voice shouting "Goal!" He thought he was dreaming at first, but then the voice shouted "Goal!" again, and it sounded as if it came from the garden. Bobby jumped out of bed, went to the window and looked out. It was a bright, moonlit night, and he could see quite clearly. But you'll never guess what he did see. You won't really.

Bobby Brewster's football boots were playing football with a tennis ball on the lawn. All by themselves. One was kicking one way and one the other, and they were running all over the place. They were doing the most tricky footwork, too; at least, it wasn't exactly footwork because they hadn't got any feet in them, but it was ever so tricky! Bobby watched for a short time, then felt cold, so he went back to bed and fell asleep.

When he woke the next morning, he thought again that he may have been dreaming, but he dressed quickly and went downstairs. He looked in the cupboard, and can you guess what he saw? Two muddy football boots. He did, really.

"Well," said Bobby Brewster to himself, "there's only one explanation. They must be magic football boots."

At least he thought he said it to himself, but he can't have done, because a voice said, "We are."

"I beg your pardon?" asked Bobby Brewster.

"I said we are magic football boots," said the voice.

"You're even more magic than I thought then," said Bobby Brewster. "You can talk as well as run."

"There's nothing magic about football boots running," said the voice. "They wouldn't be much good if they couldn't."

"Perhaps not," answered Bobby Brewster, "but they usually have feet in them."

"That's true," said the voice. "Maybe I had better explain. First of all, though, we must introduce ourselves. I'm the left boot and my name's Biff. My brother on the

right is called Boff, but he can't talk."

"What a pity," said Bobby Brewster.

"Yes, it is rather," said Biff. "He's jolly good at football, though. Last night he beat me 3–2, and the game before that he won 4–0."

"It's a bit of a nuisance that you play football at night, you know," said Bobby Brewster. "I always have to go to school with muddy boots."

"That's what I'm going to explain," said Biff. "We're only playing to help you."

"How do you make that out?" asked Bobby Brewster curiously.

"After your first game at Miss Trensham's," said Biff, "you told your mother we were silly boots and that we couldn't run or kick."

"I'm very sorry," said Bobby Brewster. "I'd never have mentioned it if I'd thought you were listening."

"Boff and I were very disappointed to hear it," said

Biff, "because we'd taken a liking to you. So we decided to practise at nights until we were really good at football. Then you could play better in us, and you wouldn't need to complain any more."

"That was most thoughtful of you," said Bobby Brewster. "And, you know, I'm much better at football already."

"Just you wait till we've had more practice," said Biff. "You'll be the best player in the school. We're going to play every Tuesday and Friday night so that we get better and better. I'm afraid, though," he added rather sadly, "I shall never beat Boff. He's much better than I am."

"Never mind," said Bobby Brewster, "I'll try to remember to use my right foot for kicking goals."

And that's exactly what Bobby Brewster has done ever since then. It's the end of term now, and he's the best player in the school, even better than the bigger boys. He runs up the field kicking the ball first with Boff and then with Biff. When he gets near the goal, Boff! In it goes, and Miss Trensham cries, "Oh, well played, Brewster!"

There's just one thing. Instead of cleaning his boots on Mondays and Thursdays, Bobby Brewster gets up early every Wednesday and Saturday morning after Biff and Boff have been practising, and cleans them so they are ready for his next game. He polishes them especially well, and while he is doing it he makes plans with Biff for playing their next game together. Even though he can't talk, Boff must be listening, too, because the plans always seem to work.

I know what you're thinking. What will Bobby Brewster do when he grows out of his football boots and has to buy a bigger pair? I'm afraid I can't answer that question. He'll have to go into the shop and ask the manager for a pair of magic football boots. I hope they have them in stock, don't you?

This story came from "Bobby Brewster's Shadow" by H. E. Todd and there are several more books about the doings of Bobby. Look out for them in your library.

Checkpoint

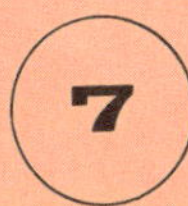

How well did you read?

On what days of the week did the boys play football?
What did Bobby think of his football boots at first?
What woke him up one night?
What was the name of the left boot?
What problem will Bobby have one day?

Choose

The words in the box are in the story.
Their meanings are in the circle.
Find the way to pair them off.

ordinary insisted impressive tactless explanation nuisance pavilion complain

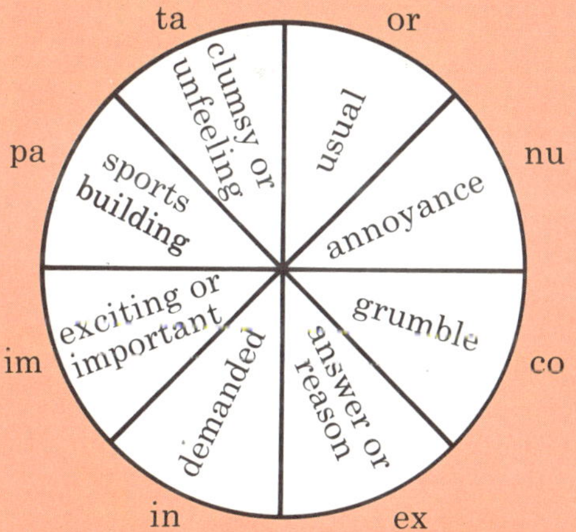

Football History

Nowadays everyone knows about football. People have their favourite teams, wear their team colours, argue about the game and watch it on television. Yet only a hundred years ago few people knew much about the game or had even seen it played. Some say it started long ago in Roman times, with a game in which two sides struggled with a piece of wood, or a kind of ball, trying to carry it over a line marked on the ground behind each side. For hundreds of years there had been wild games played by young men, who kicked and fought over a pig's bladder which had been blown up and sometimes covered with leather to make it stronger. But no one except the players liked this uproar in the streets. In fact, what with the roughness of the game, the fights that started and the damage done to property, laws were passed forbidding people to play it. King Edward II and King Richard III disliked it because it prevented young men from practising archery. Kings were always wanting soldiers and they thought that skill with the bow was more important than skill with a ball.

Yet, in spite of the laws, the game went on, although it usually moved out to the fields where it was less of a nuisance. Most players seemed to make up their own rules. This is probably what started the fights, especially as it was quite common for the spectators to join in. Oddly enough, this seems to be happening again nowadays when spectators swarm over the pitch after a game.

Just over a hundred years ago, the goal-posts had no cross-bar, although sometimes there was a rope or tape joining them. The players usually wore caps, so they could not have headed the ball very much. Perhaps this explains the saying "being capped for . . ." which is used when a player is picked to play for his country. At that time, too, the players wore peculiar trousers, called 'knickerbockers', which strapped up just below the knee. You could always tell who the referee was, because he wore a bowler hat and often carried a walking stick!

In 1863 the Football Association was formed and the clubs which belonged to it agreed to play matches against each other, keeping to a *fixed* set of rules. The size of the pitch, and the goals, and the ball, and so on were also decided upon. Football also split into two very different kinds, association football (soccer) and rugby football (rugger). The main difference between them is that in one you can handle the ball as well as kick it. It is said that the Sheffield United players wore kid gloves at first, to remind them *not* to handle the ball.

Football was a British invention and the game was spread round the world by our soldiers and sailors. People in other lands saw them enjoying themselves with the game and were soon copying them. In 1904 an International Football Association was formed, and so games between different nations took place, leading to the World Cup competition of today.

So football has progressed from a pig's bladder to the World Cup, and no doubt there will be more changes as time goes on. It is interesting to see how fashions in players' kit have altered over the years. The knicker-bockers gave way to shorts, rather long ones you may have noticed if you have seen films of old games. The massive shin guards and heavy leather football boots covering the ankles have also gone. Nowadays, shorts are very short indeed, and the boots are really lightweight shoes. All this is for speed, for the modern footballer has to be as fit and as agile as a ballet dancer.

But the game seems to be getting rougher. Maybe in a hundred years from now players will be padded all over like American footballers are today. Perhaps this would slow the game down so much that it would not be worth watching, and everyone will go sailing, or playing golf or rock-climbing. Then football will be no more.

A Tangle of Riddles

Find the riddle. Follow the line to the answer.

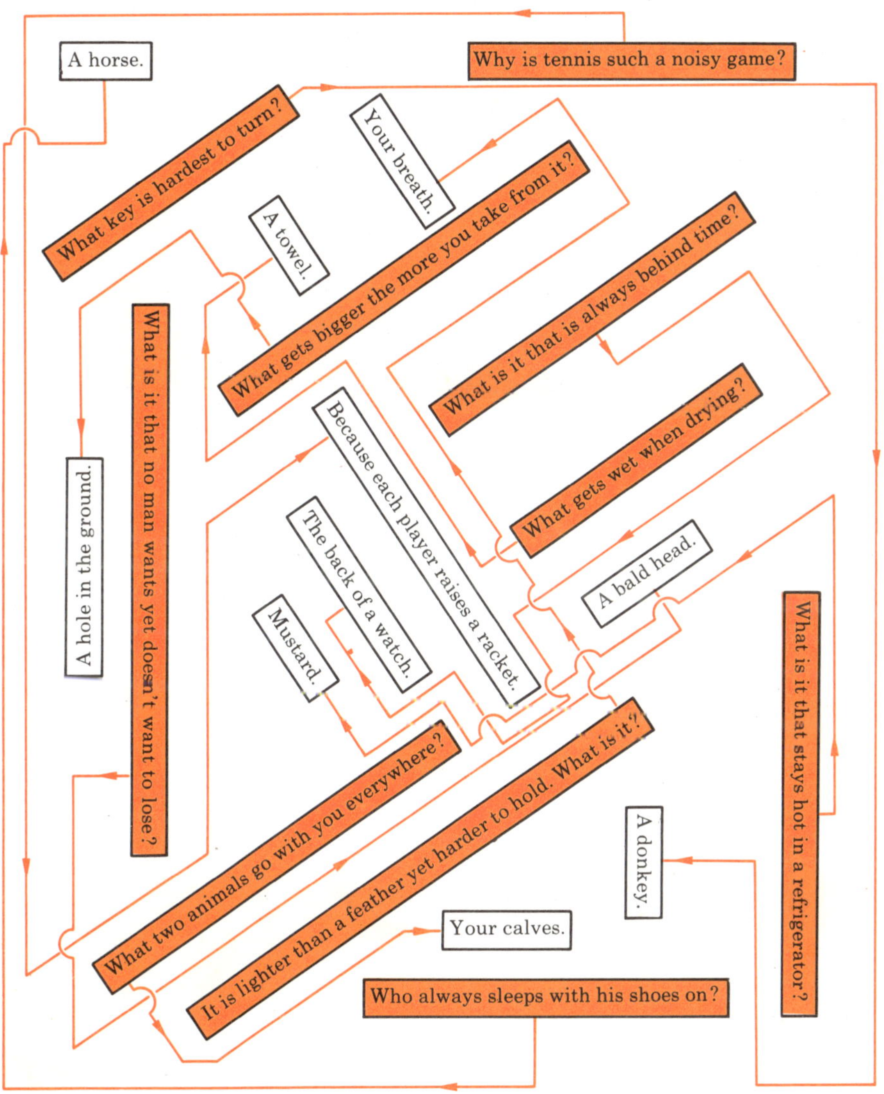

The Marvellous Tree

At first, the Caribs lived on the Moon. They stood on the surface of the Moon and gazed up at the skies around them. They saw the Sun in the daytime and millions of stars at night. Some of the stars shone steadily with a clear light and some twinkled like little lamps. Also, they saw the Earth.

There it was, up in the sky, looking quite near. It was not beautiful, though, like the stars. It was dull and dark and grey. It looked as though it needed cleaning thoroughly. So the Caribs decided to clean it.

They all mounted their chariots and rode up into the sky. They sailed through the clouds, they travelled across space, and they landed on the Earth. Then they set to work to clean it. They polished the mountains, they scrubbed the valleys, and they dusted the grass. They all worked so hard that before long the Earth was clean. It shone and sparkled just as brightly as the Sun, the Moon and the stars. They were delighted with the results of their work.

As there was no more cleaning to do, the Caribs decided to go back to their home on the Moon. When they looked round for their chariots, however, they could not see them anywhere. They had disappeared. The Caribs were stranded.

Then they discovered another thing. There was no food left. When they came from the Moon, they had brought plenty with them, but now it was all gone. They had nothing to eat.

So they began to search for food on the Earth. They searched in the valleys and on the mountains, in the forests and over the grassy plains. They even dug up pieces of clay from the ground and baked them, but the clay was nothing like bread and it was not good to eat.

Once, one of the young Caribs, who was quick to notice things, saw a tree which stood up tall and straight. Hanging from the branches were large clusters of red berries. Many birds visited the tree, perching on the branches and gobbling the berries.

Full of hope, the Caribs began picking the red berries. They tasted them and found they were delicious. They ate cluster after cluster, hoping that the berries would prove to be good food. For a while they were happy, but they soon found that though the berries were delicious, they were not good as food. The Caribs were still hungry, and now they began to grow thin.

Then, at last, God was sorry for them. He saw how thin and hungry they had grown; He saw how unhappy they were, and He decided to help them. So He created a marvellous new tree for them. It was enormous, the largest tree on Earth. Each branch not only was huge, but bore different kinds of fruit. On some branches grew great bunches of bananas. On others hung hundreds of oranges, like bright lanterns among the dark green leaves. On every branch grew something that was good to eat, and beneath the tree, in the shade of the dark leaves, there sprang up many kinds of plants. Some were maize, some were potatoes, all were good food. There was enough to feed all the Caribs, to make them happy and strong again, and still have food left over.

But the Caribs did not see the tree. It grew in the thickest part of the forest and they did not know it was there. However, somebody found the tree. It was the Wild Pig, who was always rooting about in the forest, and one day he came upon the marvellous new tree. He grunted with delight. He gobbled up as much of the food as he could, and every day he went back for more. Once he had been thin and hungry-looking, but soon he became as fat and smooth as a balloon.

The Caribs, who by now were nearly starving, noticed that the Wild Pig was growing very fat and contented. They guessed that somewhere he had discovered some new food. They tried to follow him and find it for themselves, but Wild Pig was crafty. He wanted to keep the marvellous new tree all to himself, and whenever they came after him, he crouched down in the grass and hid himself until they had gone.

The Caribs were disappointed. They talked it over and decided to get help from someone else. First, they tried the Woodpecker, for he was a very friendly bird and always ready to help people. They explained to him that Wild Pig had grown very fat lately and that he had probably found some good food. They asked Woodpecker if he could follow Wild Pig and they promised that if he could find where he got his food, he should have a share of it.

Woodpecker agreed and the next morning he set out and followed Wild Pig through the forest, flying from tree to tree. On and on they went, but Woodpecker, who was rather stupid, stopped at a tree every now and then and pecked at the bark with his big beak. He was hungry and wanted to catch a few juicy insects. Every time he pecked at the bark he made a tapping sound, and it was not long before Wild Pig heard him. The noise seemed to be following him, he thought. He grew suspicious and, looking up into the trees, he saw Woodpecker.

He realised that Woodpecker was following him and he guessed that he was helping the Caribs. So he stopped and hid in the bushes, and went no further towards the tree until it was dark and the Woodpecker could not see him.

Again the Caribs were disappointed. This time, they tried another animal. They went to see Rat and asked him to help them. Rat was not so stupid as Woodpecker, but neither was he so friendly. All the same, he agreed to follow Wild Pig.

Rat was very skilful at this kind of thing. He could move through the forest silently, without making a sound. He was hard to see, for his fur was just the same colour as the floor of the forest. He followed Wild Pig all the morning and Wild Pig never suspected he was there. At last they reached the big tree. Rat watched while Wild Pig ate the food. Then, when he had gone, Rat tried some for himself. He found it was delicious. Never had he tasted such good potatoes, such fine bananas, such juicy oranges. He slapped his stomach with joy and decided that all this marvellous food was much too good to share with the Caribs. When he had eaten all he wanted, he went back to them and said that he had lost track of Wild Pig.

Once more the Caribs were disappointed, but they asked Rat to keep trying and to follow Wild Pig every day. So every day Rat went to the wonderful tree, and he ate and ate and ate, and then every evening he returned to the Caribs and told them that he had lost track of Wild Pig.

The poor Caribs were hungrier than ever and they grew thinner and thinner. When they looked at Rat, however, they noticed that he was getting fatter and fatter every day. Once, like them, he had been hungry and thin: now he seemed quite plump, almost as fat as Wild Pig. The Caribs became suspicious. They caught hold of Rat and made him tell them the truth. Then they held him fast and forced him to lead them through the forest to the marvellous tree. When at last they reached it, they could hardly believe their eyes. They gazed at the fruit hanging in clusters from the branches and the crops growing in

the shade of the leaves, and they knelt down and thanked God for saving them from starvation.

Then they got up and went towards the tree, eager to eat its fruits. As they did so, a great voice came to them, sounding loud yet far-distant at the same time. It echoed through all the forest.

"Cut down the tree," said the great voice.

The Caribs were astonished. Why cut down such a marvellous tree? But they thought it best to obey, and with their simple tools they began chopping at the trunk. It took them a long time, but at last, with a mighty crash, the tree toppled to the ground.

Then each one of the Caribs pulled a branch from the tree. They carried the branches home and each one planted a branch in his garden. Before very long, a wonderful thing happened. Each branch grew and grew until it became a tree, and each tree sent out great clusters of oranges, bananas and other delicious fruits, and beneath each tree sprang up many fine crops and vegetables.

So, after all their struggles, the Caribs had plenty of food. Everyone had his own tree and nobody went hungry again. They lived happily on the Earth and, after a while, they quite forgot about their old home on the Moon.

That is the story. Is it true? Well, some of it is certainly not. No people, except astronauts, have ever been on the Moon, and a chariot would not be a very good way of travelling through space. Neither has any tree ever been heard of which grows oranges *and* bananas *and* other kinds of fruit, too. However, one thing at least is true. There were, and still are, people called the Caribs. They were a fierce and rather war-like people who inhabited parts of South America and the tropical islands we now call the West Indies, where some of them still live today. They gave their name to the sea near those islands, for it is called the Caribbean. And, whether it is true or not, the Caribs still enjoy telling the story of their marvellous tree to their children.

Checkpoint 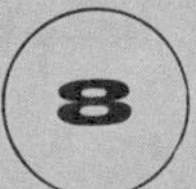

How well did you read?

Why did the Caribs leave the Moon?
Why could they not go back?
What was wrong with the red berries?
Who found the marvellous tree first?
How did the Wild Pig dodge the Woodpecker?
What did the Rat tell the Caribs at first?
What did the Caribs do to the marvellous tree?

Meanings

These ten words are in the story:

thoroughly stranded clusters created
contented crafty crouched suspicious
plump echoed

You can find their meanings by following the clues in this shape:

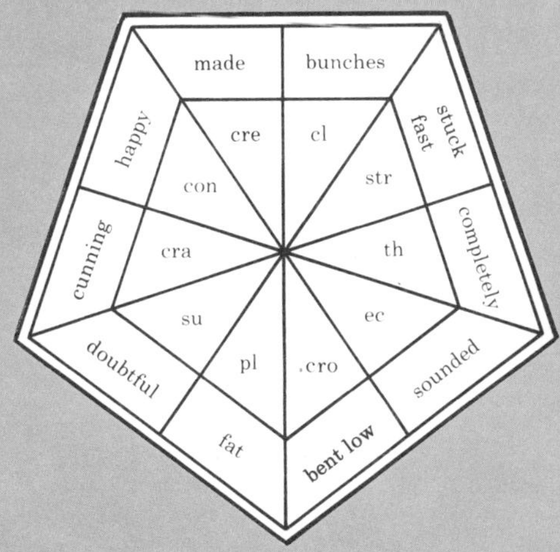

The Knapsack

There was once a soldier who had served his King and country for many years, but the last war he had fought in had done no one any good. Wars rarely do any good at any time. The King's treasure was almost exhausted. All the soldiers were sent home, with only a few copper coins as a reward for all their service and bravery. This soldier was trudging homewards with only three pennies in his pocket.

On the way he met an old woman.

"Give a poor woman a penny, kind soldier," the woman pleaded. "Just a penny."

"I've only got three pennies," said the soldier, "but there's not much difference between three pennies and two pennies. Here you are." He handed over a penny and went on his way.

Not long afterwards he came upon another old lady

sitting at the wayside holding out her apron.

"Spare a penny, kind soldier," she cried. "I am hungry."

"Bless me, another one!" exclaimed the soldier taking off his hat and scratching his head. "I've only two pennies anyway, but no matter." He handed over a penny and went on his way whistling.

Sure enough, he soon met another old lady resting on a gate.

"Why can't I meet a *young* lady for a change?" groaned the soldier to himself.

"Spare a penny, young man," implored the old lady. "Spare a penny so that I can buy some food."

"Everybody's hungry round here," sighed the soldier, for he was a patient man. "You won't get much food for a penny," he shouted, for he thought the old lady looked as if she might be deaf as well as hungry. "Do you know one penny is all I have except these clothes I stand in, and a torn shirt and a pair of socks full of holes in the knapsack on my back? But never mind. Here's your penny and you are welcome, old girl."

"Don't you ever want anything for yourself?" enquired the old lady.

"I wish for something now and again," answered the soldier. "Sometimes I get what I wish for, sometimes I don't. Mostly I don't."

"Suppose you could have anything you wished for *now*. What would you wish?" asked the old lady.

"Now that's a difficult question," said the soldier, fingering his chin.

There was a pause while he turned over the idea in his mind.

"Ah, yes!" he exclaimed at last, "I would wish that my knapsack might never wear out and whatever I asked to be put in it should remain there until I wanted it."

"Granted," said the old lady who then began to fade like a shadow when the sun goes in. The soldier raised his eyebrows and shook his head. "You certainly meet all sorts," he muttered to himself and went cheerfully on his way.

Next day he stopped at a cottage to get his water-bottle filled. A woman and her daughter were living there. They looked very miserable.

"What's the matter with you two?" asked the soldier.

"It's the landlord," answered the mother. "He wants to marry my daughter Brek here, and as we owe him many weeks' rent he says that either she marries him or he will throw us and our belongings out."

The soldier had already noticed that the young daughter was very pretty. Then he remembered his wish about the knapsack and wondered whether there was anything in the old lady's promise. Silently, he wished that his knapsack should be filled with golden coins from the landlord's money boxes. Immediately, he was pulled over backwards by the weight of his knapsack. When he had managed to slip it off and struggle to his feet, he found that underneath his torn shirt and the pair of socks full of holes the knapsack was stuffed with gold coins.

"Here you are," he said to the woman and her daughter.

"Have a few handfuls of these. They will more than pay the rent and much else besides. I must go into the town to get some new clothes. I'll stop at the inn overnight, then I'll come back when I am fitted out."

Off went the soldier to the town, and he headed for the most expensive inn he could see. It was a place where only the wealthiest people of the town came. The innkeeper looked quite annoyed to see a dusty, unkempt common soldier come through the door and seat himself at a table. Some of the other people there pulled long faces and sniffed.

"What do you want here?" asked the innkeeper haughtily.

"I want the best meal you can provide," ordered the

soldier loudly, "and I want it quickly. Jump to it, man!"

"You want what?" roared the innkeeper, his eyes bulging at the idea of having this dust-covered, travel-stained, rough-necked soldier on his premises.

"You heard," barked the soldier. "Don't judge a man by his overcoat. Catch!" And he tossed five gold coins to the innkeeper.

Now five gold coins in those days was enough money to feed about ten hungry people for a fortnight. The innkeeper quickly changed his tune. Here was a customer with money to spend, even though he looked rough and poor. Some of his regular customers never seemed to have money in their silk trousers. There was a great hustling of servants, clean table-cloths and silver cutlery appeared, and soon the dusty soldier was eating to his complete satisfaction.

The innkeeper approached when he saw that the soldier had finished his meal and, bowing low, asked if there was anything else the soldier desired.

"Yes, there is," answered the soldier, "a room for the night. Tomorrow I have to buy new clothes."

The innkeeper's face fell.

"I'm terribly sorry," he said (and he meant it), "but all our rooms have been taken except one. The great Fair begins tomorrow and there are many visitors to the town."

"Well, what's wrong with the one you *have* got?" asked the soldier. The innkeeper shuffled his feet uneasily.

"That room cannot be used," he answered.

"Cannot be used," echoed the soldier. "Why not?"

The innkeeper looked very uncomfortable.

"It is haunted," he said. "All the people who have slept in that room have been frightened almost to death during the night, and terrible noises have been heard there."

"Just the room for me!" the soldier exclaimed cheerfully. "Make it ready, please."

In spite of the innkeeper's protests and the worried looks of the servants, he insisted on occupying the haunted room. At bedtime he bade everyone a cheerful goodnight and went up the stairs to his room, whistling happily as usual.

When he got there he locked the door behind him, and put his knapsack in a corner, after taking out all the gold coins. Then, instead of undressing and getting into bed, he sat on a chair, folded his arms, crossed his legs and waited.

Soon there was scraping and banging in the chimney and presently a black sooty ball rolled out of the fireplace into the room. It unfolded into a long-haired, ugly creature with a tail and finger nails like claws.

"Hello, hello!" said the soldier. "Are there any more like you up the chimney?"

There was a great hubbub in the chimney followed by the arrival of two more sooty balls which unfolded into extremely revolting creatures. The three creatures (goodness knows what they were!) pranced about making horrible noises, but the soldier was quite calm. He just yawned as if he was watching a rather boring stage show.

"I wish you were in my knapsack," he said at last, and in an instant the sooty creatures had disappeared into the knapsack and the soldier had fastened the straps.

He then went to bed and began to snore loudly. The innkeeper, who was keeping an ear open for blood-curdling screams, was astonished. The snores continued

until late in the morning. When they ceased, the innkeeper went up with the soldier's breakfast. He could hardly believe his eyes. The soldier had clearly had a very good night's sleep and was more than ready for his breakfast.

"Ah, innkeeper!" said the soldier, "my knapsack is very dusty. Have it sent to the blacksmith and ask him to place it on his anvil and beat it with the largest hammer he has. Then it is to be opened and emptied out."

The innkeeper had never heard of knapsacks being beaten before. He moved across the room to pick it up. He couldn't shift it. He had to send for two servants to lift it.

"This is as heavy as the Devil," observed one servant.

"Perhaps he's inside," joked the other.

When it arrived at the blacksmith's there was no delay. The blacksmith was delighted because he had received a gold coin in advance and he set to work with tremendous enthusiasm and vigour.

The soldier came along to watch. When he thought the beating had gone on long enough he ordered the blacksmith to empty the bag.

Only a large pile of soot fell out. What had happened to the three creatures? Well, they certainly never went back to the chimney. As for the soldier, he fitted himself out with a splendid set of new clothes, including several shirts and lots of socks without holes in them. He then went off to marry the pretty girl at the cottage. But he always took great care of his knapsack, for this gave him almost everything he needed. This was his reward for being kind to old ladies. Maybe that's worth remembering!

Checkpoint

How well did you read?

What did the soldier have in his knapsack?
Why did the woman and her daughter look miserable?
Why were there many visitors in the town?
What advice did the soldier give the innkeeper?
What did the innkeeper expect to hear during the night?
The last sentence says: "Maybe that's worth remembering!" What is?

Make sure of these words

exhausted ♡1	cutlery ♧1
trudging ◇1	protests ◇3
pleaded ♤1	hubbub ♤2
implored ♤1	revolting ♧2
provide ♡1	pranced ♤3
premises ◇2	vigour ♡3

Check
the meanings by matching the signs.

complaints ◇3 strength and energy ♡3 jumped about ♤3
spent, worn out, empty ♡1 disgusting ♧2 begged ♤1
knives ♧1 walking wearily ◇1 uproar and din ♤2
buildings ◇2 supply ♡1

Little Bits of Paper

It is just a tiny bit of paper, about two centimetres square. When it was first made it cost only one penny. Now it is worth thousands of pounds. What is it? It is a postage stamp.

Not just any old postage stamp, of course. This one comes from Mauritius, a little island in the Indian Ocean. It was printed in 1847 and is orange-red in colour. A used envelope with two of these stamps stuck in one corner was sold for 375 000 dollars in New York in 1968. That's about £200 000!

Why is such a small piece of paper worth so much money? It is because there are thousands and thousands of people all over the world who collect stamps. Above all they like to collect stamps which are rare and they are willing to pay a high price for them. There are not many of these Mauritius stamps in the world, so they are very rare and very, very valuable.

Most stamps are not rare at all. There are plenty of them in the world, so they are not valuable. You can buy them quite cheaply. So you do not need to be rich to be a stamp collector.

If you start a collection, tell your friends and relations about it, particularly if any of them live in other countries. Then they will save any interesting stamps they get and give them to you, unless, of course, they happen to collect stamps, too! You can buy all sorts of stamps at a stamp collector's shop.

You will soon find that you have more than one stamp of the same kind. These are called *duplicates*. The best thing to do is to find someone else who collects stamps and exchange some of your duplicates for some of his.

Where can you keep your stamps? The best plan is to fix them in a specially made book called a 'stamp album'. Sometimes, these have a page for each country and pictures of stamps, too. If you cannot have a proper album, it is almost as good to use a plain exercise book and write the name of each country at the top of each page.

When you first start, sort all your stamps into piles, with a pile for each country, and then begin the job of fixing them in the album. Do *not* stick them in with paste. Buy some special 'stamp mounts' and find out how to use them. Arrange your stamps carefully on the pages, so that they are tidy and attractive.

Look at each stamp through a magnifying glass. You will be surprised by the interesting things you may find. Look at their shapes. You will find squares, rectangles and triangles, of course, but what about circles? Are there any? If not, why not?

Most postage stamps, though not all, show the name of their country. Do British stamps give a name, and if not, how will you know they are British? Some stamps from other lands use names which are strange to us. Spanish stamps usually have the word ESPAÑA and this means SPAIN. Swiss stamps have the word HELVETIA and this means SWITZERLAND, while stamps from SWEDEN have the word SVERIGE. Dutch stamps use the word for HOLLAND which is NEDERLAND.

Another thing you can learn from stamps is the kind of money which each country uses — *pence* in Britain, *cents* in the United States of America, *pfennigs* and *Deutsche Marks* in Western Germany, while in France stamps are marked in *centimes*.

Most countries show a picture of some kind on their stamps. Sometimes, it is a picture of the chief person in that country. It often used to be a king, but there are not many kings about nowadays. Sometimes the picture is of a famous person, like Columbus or Winston Churchill.

Many stamps show pictures of animals. There are horses, lions, tigers, elephants, fish and even prehistoric animals. There are kangaroos, koala bears and emus from Australia, springboks from South Africa, buffalo from America and leopards from Zaire. In fact, you can find

enough animals to make your album into a stamp zoo.

There is plenty of sport shown on stamps, too. Some countries have special stamps printed at the time of the Olympic Games. There have been pictures of English cricketers on West Indian stamps and when the Soccer World Cup series was played in England in 1966 special stamps were issued.

Sometimes, important events of the past or the present are shown on stamps. When men first landed on the Moon, the stamps of the United States of America showed an astronaut climbing out of his spaceship on to the surface of the moon. Russia also printed pictures of a spaceship on its stamps. But sometimes the event pictured happened long, long ago. Nine hundred years after the Battle of Hastings, British stamps were sold showing pictures of the battle.

Although people have been writing letters to each other for thousands of years, stamps have not been in use for so very long. The world's first postage stamps were printed in Britain in 1840, less than two hundred years ago. They cost one penny each and bore a picture of Queen Victoria, who was queen at the time. They were black stamps and have always been called *'penny blacks'*. They are worth more than a penny now. Other countries liked the idea and started printing their own stamps. Now there are many thousands of different kinds. There are many thousands of stamp collectors in the world, too, so many that they have been given a special name. They are called *philatelists* and their albums are crammed with rather special 'little bits of paper'.

The Teapot Badger

You are not likely to meet a badger on a country walk. This is not because there aren't any about, but because they are usually sound asleep during the daytime and wander about only at night. Whenever they do come out they always seem to enjoy themselves immensely.

Long ago, a certain badger in Japan was having a fine time early one evening. He was rolling over and over on the grass, turning somersaults and banging his stomach with his paws like someone who had just enjoyed a good meal. In fact, he was enjoying himself so much that in the long grass he didn't notice a bamboo bent over holding a noose of rope. It was a trap set by someone to catch wild animals. The noose slipped over the badger's shoulders, the bent bamboo stick sprang upright and poor badger was held fast. He rushed hither and thither but the noose only became tighter as he struggled. He began to scream with terror.

But help was close at hand, for just then a tinker was passing on his way home after a day's work. Well, you are not likely to come across a tinker nowadays either. They are about as rare as badgers. They used to travel around mending pots and pans. This particular Japanese tinker was trudging home with a large bamboo basket on his back. In it were all his tools and bits and pieces. He heard the cries of the poor badger and ran to search in the long grass.

"Oya, Oya, Oya!" he said. "A little badger in a trap. Come along, my beauty." He loosened the noose from the badger's neck and set him free.

"Well, my fine fellow," he said, stroking the badger's ruffled fur and patting him. "Off you go and be more careful in the future."

The badger was surprised by the tinker's kindness, for kindness to animals in those days, and even sometimes in these days, was rare.

"Eah, eah, arg," he said, which really meant, "How can I repay you?" But, of course, the tinker did not understand that and said, "Off you go." He pulled his bamboo basket closer to his back and started towards his home once again.

The badger stood watching him going down the road wondering what he could do to reward his rescuer. Now it seems that Japanese badgers in those days had certain magical powers. These powers were different for different badgers. This badger had but one magical power which he knew of, but which he had always thought to be rather silly and useless. Now a bright idea struck him and he saw how he could reward the tinker. So calling up his magic power he slowly began to change himself into a beautiful silver teapot.

His body grew fatter and rounder. His four paws grew gradually smaller and his pointed and whiskery nose began to change into a spout. But, before he had completely changed, he managed to leap on to the tinker's basket and hide inside.

When the tinker approached his house, his wife came to greet him. The setting sun must have sent a silver gleam from the teapot spout sticking out from the basket and it caught her eye.

"Goodness!" she exclaimed. "What is this? A silver teapot. Where did you get it?"

The tinker was speechless with astonishment. He knew nothing about the silver teapot or how it had got into his basket.

They took it carefully into their little house and set it down on the bare planking of the floor. There its silver shone brightly against the dull wood. Its beautiful shape reminded them of the beauty of a sleek animal. They knelt beside it in silent admiration.

"I have never, never seen such a beautiful teapot!" exclaimed the wife. "Where did you get it? You *must* know."

"Indeed I don't," replied her puzzled husband. "I have never set eyes upon it before."

They both sat silently for a time enchanted by the beauty of the silver teapot. Then the tinker spoke.

"You know, wife," he said quietly, "it is too good for humble folk such as us. I think we should offer it to the temple, for that is the place where the greatest treasures are."

"Yes, indeed," replied his wife. "The priest will surely welcome this for the Great Tea Ceremony."

You must understand that at the time of this story the Japanese temples held important ceremonies or services which included special ways of making and drinking tea, for tea was, and still is, a highly honoured drink in Japan.

So the tinker and his wife wrapped the teapot carefully in cloth and went to the temple. The priest was not only surprised to see such a beautiful teapot, but even more surprised to hear that the tinker had no idea how he came by it. After a good deal of talking, the priest decided there was no way of finding out who the real owner was. He said he would accept it into the temple's treasury.

When the tinker and his wife had returned to their home, the priest sat examining the remarkable teapot more closely.

"It is indeed a lovely teapot," he murmured to himself. "I cannot wait until the Great Tea Ceremony to use it. I will have a special small ceremony tonight and invite a few guests."

So, that evening, the priest and his guests laid out the small stove and the cups at the door of the temple and sat round in a circle. The priest filled the teapot with water and placed it on the stove to boil. Almost at once there was a loud cry of pain. "Too hot! Too hot!" and to everyone's amazement the teapot rolled off the stove with a bump and much spilling of water. Its shape seemed to change. Did not the spout begin to look like a nose, and the handle like a tail, and the four short legs grow longer and move? Indeed they did. For the teapot charged round the room leaving a trail of steam behind it and shouting "Too hot! Too hot!" all the time.

The priest fell over backwards yelling, "It's a ghost! It's bewitched!" People from other parts of the temple, hearing the noise, came rushing in.

"Where's the ghost?" they asked. "What's happened?"

The priest was quite shaken and he pointed a trembling finger at the teapot, which was now in a corner looking just as a very beautiful teapot should look. The onlookers poked it gently with broomsticks but nothing happened and soon they went away thinking that the priest and his guests must have been dreaming. The priest was so upset that he thought the best thing to do was to return the teapot to the tinker. The very next day he went to the tinker's home and said that on second thoughts he felt the tinker ought to have the teapot back.

The tinker and his wife were quite pleased with this and, just before they went to sleep for the night, they had another close look at it and then left it on the pillow.

During the night they were awakened by a voice. "Tinker, tinker," it said, "Wake up."

The couple rubbed their eyes and were startled to see a badger sitting on their pillow.

"It's all right, it's all right," said the badger. "I am the badger you rescued from the trap and I was very grateful. But I spoke to you in my own language and you went on your way not understanding that I wanted to reward you for your kindness." He went on to explain that he had one magic power only, which he had always thought rather silly and useless. It was to be able to change himself into a teapot. In fact, he could arrange things so that he could be half badger and half teapot. This he had done in the temple to trick the priest because he wanted to get back to the tinker. He did not think the tinker would be so unselfish as to give him away with no benefit to himself.

"Now," said the badger, "watch this."

The tinker and his wife sat in bed and watched an astonishing spectacle. The badger changed to half teapot and half badger and gave a breathtaking display of acrobatics all round the room. Then he told the tinker and his wife what to do.

The very next day they went to the market place and built a small stage inside a tent. Outside it they put up a huge notice with many coloured flags flying round it. On it was printed in large Japanese letters:

THE PERFORMING TEAPOT
THE ONLY TEAPOT IN THE WORLD
THAT
WALKS DANCES AND DOES CARTWHEELS

This caused quite a hubbub in the market place and soon crowds gathered round anxious to see this great wonder. There were farmers with their wives, mothers with their babies, and children of all shapes and sizes jostling and jabbering with excitement all wondering what a performing teapot would look like.

Suddenly the curtains parted to show the tinker kneeling in the centre of the stage, bowing low as was the Japanese custom. Then in came the badger-teapot to bow low to the audience also. The audience was speechless. A walking teapot that bowed! There was a great buzz of chatter and talk.

The tinker raised his hand for silence and said,

"Honourable people. The rare and wonderful performing teapot will now dance."

So the badger-teapot began his show which included somersaults and walking the tightrope. The crowd was delighted. There was tremendous applause and stamping of feet. In no time at all the fame of the teapot spread and the tinker moved from village to village with the badger and people flocked to see the show. It was not long before the tinker and his wife were quite rich.

But they were not greedy folk and one day the tinker said to the badger, "My friend, you have more than repaid me for helping you. We are now rich and we can live contentedly for the rest of our lives. Is it not time you returned to your own home in the forest?"

As a matter of fact, the badger *was* rather tired and beginning to think about the home he had left, and he was glad to be given the chance to go back home.

"Carry me back to the place where you found me," he said, "and there we will part."

The badger changed to a complete teapot and the tinker and his wife wrapped him up lovingly and carried him back to the woods. It was rather a sad little gathering there. They unwrapped the teapot which slowly, and perhaps rather unwillingly, changed back into a handsome badger. They did not say "goodbye"; they just bowed to each other, and in an instant the tinker and his wife were alone with only the sound of the wind in the trees for company.

Checkpoint 

Half of all the words on this page are in the story. The other half are words that mean much the same. Your task is to pair them off or find their partners. Some signs have been given as clues to help you, but make sure you examine the signs carefully because some are almost alike.

immensely gradually noose

somersault completely sparkle

praise little by little profit, gain

gleam sleek altogether greatly

admiration head over heels benefit

spectacle loop show smooth

ceremony

Yes, there is an odd one over.
Which is it? How many kinds of it can you think of?

A Scatter of Riddles

Find the question, then the answer.

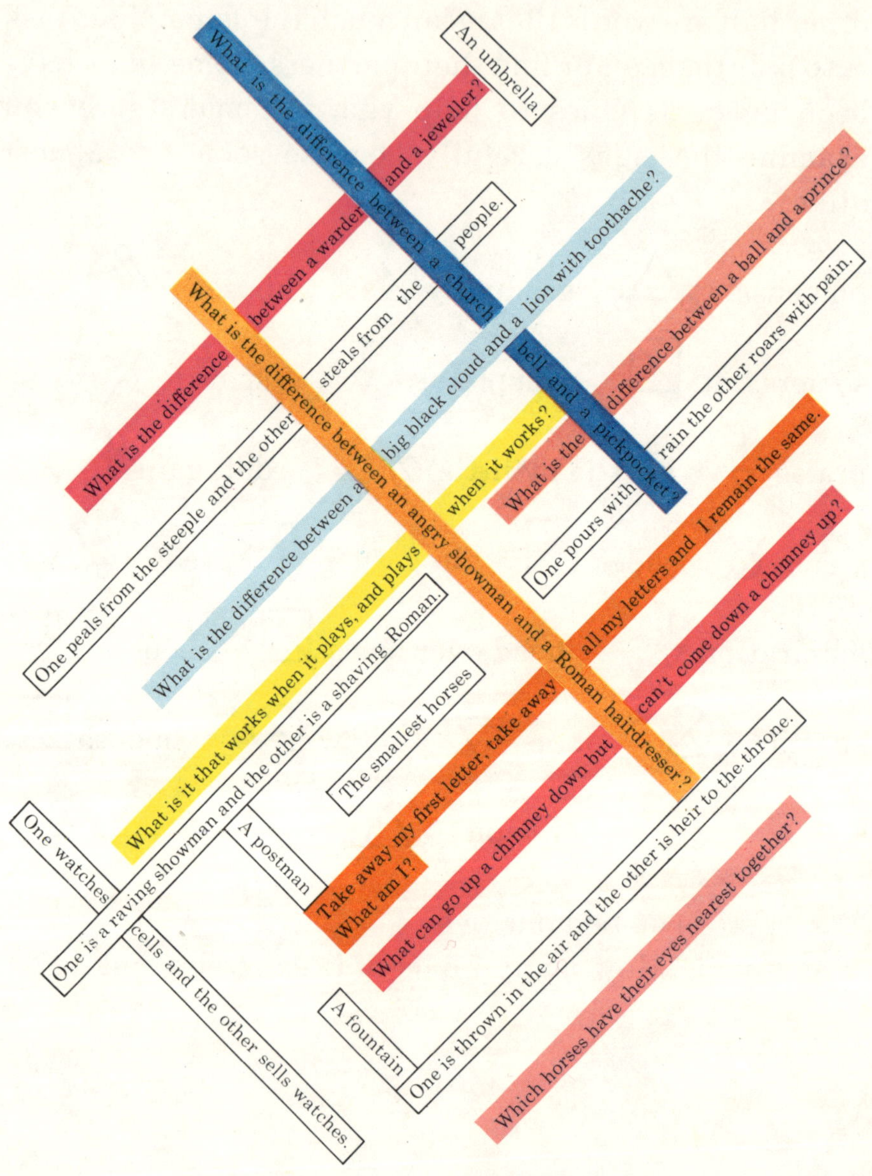

Anansi and Tiger

Tiger was king of the forest. We should have called him a leopard, because he had spots, not stripes; but everyone in the forest called him Tiger. He was the largest, strongest and fiercest of the animals there. All the others were very polite to Tiger and extremely careful not to offend him.

As he was so important, they named many things after him. For instance, all the stories that the animals told round the fire in an evening were called Tiger Stories.

The weakest, smallest animal in the forest was the spider, Anansi. No one thought that Anansi was important at all. Nothing was named after him.

This worried Anansi. He wished he was more important. So one evening he went to see Tiger.

"Excuse me, Tiger," he said, bowing low, "but I wondered if you would do me a favour."

At first, Tiger took no notice, so Anansi said it again. "I wondered if you would please do me a favour."

Then Tiger looked down at him in his proud way, and after a while he said, "What favour is this, Anansi?"

"Well, it's like this," said Anansi. "Everyone in the forest names things after you, but I am not important so no one ever names anything after me."

"I see," said Tiger grandly. "And I suppose you think that something should be named after you instead."

"Yes," replied Anansi in his small voice. "Yes, please, Tiger. I should like all the stories to be named after me. I should like them to be called Anansi Stories."

"Oh, you would, would you?" said Tiger, looking extremely grim. For he was very fond of stories and he liked them to be named after him. He certainly had no intention of letting them be called Anansi Stories.

So he said, "Well now, Anansi, I suppose I might do you this favour, but only if you will do me *two* favours first."

Anansi knew there would be a catch in it somewhere. Tiger did not do anyone favours if he could help it.

"What favours must I do then?" asked Anansi, feeling sure that they would be something difficult.

"Oh, nothing much," said Tiger, smiling grimly. "First, just catch me a gourd full of live bees."

The alligator, who was resting in the grass near by, heard this and chuckled to himself. The monkey, hanging in the bough of a tree, heard it and screamed with laughter. Anansi thought to himself, "How on earth can I do that? The bees will not go into the gourd. They will sting me."

"The second favour," went on Tiger, still smiling coldly, "is to bring me Mr Snake. Bring him to me alive, please. I'll give you a week to do these two things, Anansi. Then, if you succeed, the stories can all be named after you, just as you ask."

Again the alligator and the monkey laughed to themselves, and Anansi thought, "How on earth can I capture Mr Snake? He's much bigger than I am. He won't come and he'll probably eat me."

"Very well, Tiger," he replied, as cheerfully as he could, "I'll do what you ask," but when he looked round, Tiger had stalked off, proudly and silently, into the forest.

Now a gourd, in case you don't know, is a very large fruit. People eat the inside and sometimes use the empty rind as a bottle. There were plenty about in the forest and Anansi soon found one. He carried it along with him through the trees. Many animals saw him and wondered what he was doing. The ant asked him, and the lizard asked him, and the centipede asked him, but he did not answer them. Then the Queen Bee came buzzing along, and she asked him, too.

"Well, you see," said Anansi, "Tiger bet me I could not

tell him how many bees a gourd could hold. I have no idea, and I know I shall lose the bet. Can't you help me?"

"No, I can't," replied the Queen Bee, "I don't know the answer any more than you do. Can't you work it out by a sum?"

"No," sighed Anansi, "I'm no good at division."

Queen Bee could not think of any more good advice to give, so she flew away, but before long she came back and brought with her a swarm of her bees. Anansi was looking sad and muttering to himself, "How many bees? How many bees?"

Queen Bee seemed excited. "It's all right, Anansi," she cried, "I've thought of a way. All you have to do is to open the gourd and hold it up. Then I and my bees will fly into it. As we go in you must count us. Then, when the gourd is full, you'll know exactly how many bees it will hold."

"A splendid idea," said Anansi happily. "I don't know how you thought of it."

So that is what they did. Anansi took out the cork and in flew the bees, one after the other. Anansi counted all the time and when he got to "one hundred and fifty-four" the gourd was full, so he put the cork in and they could not get out. Then he struggled through the forest with the heavy gourd till he found Tiger.

"Here it is, Tiger," he called, "a gourd full of bees. There are one hundred and fifty-four of them, all alive."

Tiger was not in the least pleased. He never thought Anansi could do it. Still, there was the second favour to be

done: that would be much too hard for him.

"That was the easy one," said Tiger. "Now fetch me Mr Snake, and fetch him alive." Tiger chuckled to himself as he thought how clever he had been. Anansi would never capture Mr Snake in a million years.

Next day, Anansi woke early and worked very hard trying to catch Mr Snake. First he made a rope from vines and shaped it into a noose. He hung the noose near Snake's path and just beyond the noose he placed some ripe bananas. Then he held the other end of the vine rope and waited.

Soon along came Mr Snake, sliding and slithering. He saw the bananas. He hurried towards them and began to go through the noose. That was just what Anansi was waiting for. He pulled and pulled on the rope, so that the noose would tighten and catch Snake. But however hard he pulled, he could not tighten the noose. Snake was much too heavy. He just ate the bananas and then slithered and squirmed away. He had not even felt the noose.

But Anansi did not give up. He dug a deep hole in Snake's path. He smeared the sides with coconut oil so that they were very slippery, and he threw a fat, delicious pear down to the bottom of the hole. Then he hid in a bush and waited.

Soon, Snake came gliding down the path. He found the hole. He saw the ripe pear at the bottom of it, and he was just going down to get it when he noticed that the sides were slippery. If he went down there he would not be able to climb out. However, he loved fat, delicious pears, so he curled his tail round and round a nearby tree stump, lowered the rest of his body into the hole and ate up the pear. Then he pulled himself out by his tail and went on his way, leaving Anansi in the bush feeling really cross.

But still Anansi would not give up. He thought of yet another plan. He found a thin bamboo tree and bent it down to the earth. He fastened a noose to the end, so that it would fly up if it were touched. He fetched an egg, the only egg he had, and he put it just inside the noose, and he sat and waited. He knew that Snake adored eggs.

Along slithered Snake, put his slender head through and ate the egg without even touching the noose. He squirmed away, feeling by now rather full after his meal of bananas, pear and egg.

By this time, Anansi began to think that he would never catch Mr Snake. He decided to have one more try. The next day, he got out his sword and he marched along to where Snake lived. Snake was at home.

As he drew near, Anansi began to feel nervous. Snake was rather large, rather fierce. He felt even more nervous when Snake suddenly popped his head out, saw him, and called, "Hi there, man! I'm not pleased with you. I hear you've been trying to capture me. That's not friendly, man. I think I'll have to eat you."

"Don't eat me," said Anansi quickly, "it's all Tiger's fault. I had a bet with him about you."

"What was the bet?" asked Snake, getting interested.

"I said you were the longest snake in the world," said Anansi. "I said you were even longer than the tall bamboo down by the river. Tiger said you weren't."

"Of course I am, man," said Snake, who was proud of his length. "Tiger is stupid."

"I don't know," said Anansi cunningly, "now I come to look at you, I can see that you're not really quite as tall as the bamboo tree."

"I am! I am!" cried Snake, feeling furious. "Go and cut down the bamboo and put it beside me. Then you'll see that I am longer."

So Anansi went down to the river, cut down the tallest bamboo pole, brought it back and laid it down on the ground beside Snake.

Anansi then said, "Mr Snake, this is very difficult. I agree that you are very long, but when I go up to your head I think that you crawl forward and when I go down to your tail I think that you crawl backward. I don't think you are really as long as the bamboo. Tiger has won the bet after all."

"I *am* longer!" insisted Snake. "If you tie my tail to one end of the bamboo I shan't be able to move. Then you'll see that I'm longer."

So Anansi tied his tail to one end. Then he tied his middle to the middle of the bamboo, too, so that he could not possibly cheat.

"Now, let's see," said Anansi. "Yes, you're nearly as long as the bamboo. Just stretch out a little more and we shall win."

So Mr Snake took a deep breath, shut his eyes, and stretched and stretched and stretched.

"Hooray!" cried Anansi, "You've done it. You're longer than the bamboo," and quickly, before Mr Snake could even open his eyes, he tied his head to the bamboo.

Back through the forest struggled Anansi, pulling Mr Snake who was still tied to the bamboo. The alligator was surprised to see him. So was the monkey. But you can

guess who was the most surprised of all.

That is why the stories in the forest were ever afterwards called Anansi Stories.

This story and the story called "The Marvellous Tree" come from the West Indies. If you would like to read more stories like them, you will find some in a book called "West Indian Folk Tales", retold by Philip Sherlock, published by Oxford University Press.

Checkpoint

How well did you read?

What was unusual about Tiger?
Why was everyone polite to him?
How did Queen Bee help Anansi?
What three traps did Anansi set for Mr Snake?
How did Mr Snake get the pear?
What was Mr Snake very proud of?

Meanings

The words in 'boxes' come from the story.
The words in 'rings' are their meanings.
But which go together? There are clues to help you.

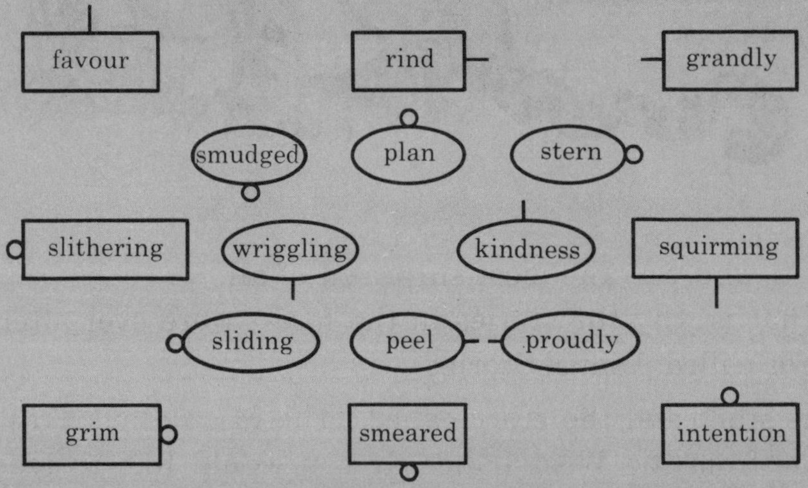

A Tiger in the House

Here comes your cat. Someone has let it in at the back door. In it comes, padding on its soft paws and glad to get in out of the cold. Mother gives it a saucer of warm milk. It purrs and drinks it all up, lapping with its pink tongue. Then it goes to the fireside. You stroke its smooth, soft fur and it settles down on the rug, enjoying the warm fire. Soon it is fast asleep. How sweet and peaceful it looks!

But suppose for a moment that it invited some of its cousins into your house and brought some of its relations to stay with it. Not just the cats from next door or down the road, but some of the other members of the cat-tribe from all over the world. Would they all be as sweet as it is? Would your house be peaceful for long?

You might find a leopard, with its black spots, stretched out on your settee. A cheetah, the swiftest animal in the world, might come striding down the hall on its long legs, while the great tawny lion, king of the beasts but rather lazy, might find your bed a good place to sleep on. The lynx, with its tufted ears, might sit in Father's favourite armchair, and, hearing a noise at the front door, you might open it to find the fiercest cat of them all, the great striped tiger, waiting to come in and join its relations.

For they are all of them members of the great cat family,

and there are more besides. There is the puma, which crouches in the branches of trees, waiting to jump on its prey. There is the savage black panther, which will attack without warning. There is the wildcat, which can still be found in lonely, far-off places in Scotland.

Just as people in the same family are rather alike, the members of the great cat family are alike, too. They are all meat-eaters and they all like to go hunting for their food. Some are happy to catch a mouse or a sparrow, but others need something bigger, like a deer or an antelope. They have very strong teeth, arranged in the same pattern, with four long, sharp fangs at the front of their mouths. Their tongues are rough and covered with very small hooks, which help them to lick meat off a bone. They have long, round tails which help them to balance, and also show when they are excited or angry. They have long, strong bodies. They are good at jumping and climbing.

They walk on their toes, very silently. They are all rather intelligent animals.

Every one of them is wild, fierce and difficult to tame — except the household cat. So how is it that cats have become so friendly? Why are they so tame and why do they love to live in our houses? No one knows for sure, but cats were once wild, too, just like lions and tigers, and their chief food was rats and mice. Now rats and mice usually live in or near people's houses, so that they can steal food. Cats probably got into the houses, too, to hunt them. The people, who found the rats and mice a nuisance, were pleased to have cats in the house. They made friends with them and the cats have stayed ever since.

The people who lived in Egypt long ago liked cats very much. Every family, rich and poor alike, kept cats. They loved their pets and punished anyone who ill-treated them. They made little models of cats and carved statues out of wood, bronze or even gold. They made necklaces out of little figures of cats, and wore cat brooches. When the family cat died, everyone was sad. They wrapped the cat's body in silk, placed it in a beautiful case of wood or bronze, and buried it. They even worshipped cats! At a place in Egypt called Bubastes, they built a temple to the goddess of the moon. They named the goddess Bastet, or Pasht, and when they painted a picture or made a statue of her, they gave her a woman's body but a cat's head. At her temple many family cats were buried.

In England a thousand years ago, cats were so useful that laws were made to stop anyone hurting them. A kitten cost one penny before its eyes were open but two pence after it had caught its first mouse. Anyone who stole a cat had to pay a large sum of money as a fine.

Then, in the times we call the Middle Ages, about six hundred years ago, there came a change. Instead of being loved, cats were feared and even hated. People thought they were bad magic. Witches were supposed to have cats. People said they had seen witches ride on cats or take them on their broomsticks when they flew up into the sky. Witches, they said, could turn themselves into cats. The worst cats were the black ones. They were very unlucky. During these times, cats did not have very happy lives and were often ill-treated.

At last, these silly ideas were forgotten. Once more, cats were taken into houses as pets. They were given milk to drink and comfortable places to sleep. There was usually a shop in every town called the 'cat's meat shop'. There was also the 'cat's meat man' who walked the streets calling out "Cat's Meat, Cat's Meat-O!" For a penny you could buy scraps of meat on a wooden skewer. Every cat recognised his voice and made tracks for home. Nowadays we usually get our cat-food in tins. More convenient, perhaps, but not so exciting for the cats.

There are over twelve million cats in Britain. Most of them are handsome, clean and loving pets, but they are still meat-hunters, and if your pet were twenty times larger, then you really would have *a tiger in the house*.

Cosy Cat Nap

Pussy-kitten, pussy-cat,
purring on the kitchen mat;
how I like your furry tail
curl'd around you like a snail.

Pussy-kitten, pussy-cat,
purring on the kitchen mat;
fire tinkles in the grate,
clocks tick tip-toe, very late.

Pussy-kitten, pussy-cat,
purring on the kitchen mat;
hear the iron softly stamp
on steaming washing, warm and damp.

Pussy-kitten, pussy-cat,
purring on the kitchen mat;
squeeze your eyes right out of sight,
and doze and blink and doze all night!

Pussy-kitten, pussy-cat,
purring on the kitchen mat;
purroo, purroo,
purroo, purroo . . . . . .

Pussy-kitten, pussy-cat,
purrooing on the kitchen mat.

James Kirkup

A Bridge to get Across

The caveman came to the river. He wanted to get across. On the other side there were woods where he often went hunting. He wanted to get to the woods.

Usually it was easy to cross the river. It was not a wide river, though it was too wide to jump. Sometimes it was not deep and the caveman could wade across. The water only came up to his knees.

Today, it was different. It had been raining hard all night and now the river was in flood. The water came right up to the top of the bank, rushing along swiftly. The caveman could not wade across today.

Further along the river there were stepping stones. They were dotted across the river and sometimes the caveman used them to cross, stepping over from one flat stone to another. But he knew it was no use going along to them today. They would be under water.

He stood on the bank, wondering what to do. It looked as though he would have to go back. Then he noticed that not far away, along the bank, there was a fallen tree. It was not very big but he thought the trunk might just reach across the river from one bank to the other.

He seized the tree and dragged it to the river. He pushed it out until the end rested on the other bank. It was just long enough. Then, balancing very carefully, he

crept along the trunk and reached the other side.

The caveman had made a bridge!

He left it there and, after that day, he always used it for crossing the river. It saved him from getting his feet wet. Once, he lost his balance and fell in. So the next day he found two more tree trunks and laid them by the side of the first one. This made the bridge wider and he did not fall in again. He was very proud of his bridge. He showed it to the other cavemen and said they could use it.

In other places, too, other cavemen had trouble in crossing rivers. Some of them were not so lucky. They had no trees nearby to use as bridges. They had to find something else.

Sometimes they used pieces of flat stone. Usually, these were not as long as a tree trunk, so they had to use two. They threw a big stone into the middle of the river first and rested the ends of the flat stones on it. In doing this they had made a bridge with two *spans*.

In other parts of the world, men used other ways of building bridges. In the thick forests of the hottest parts of the world, they made rope bridges which swung out far above deep river valleys. The ropes were made from long vines and creepers which they twisted together.

Everyone found bridges very useful. They could reach new and better hunting grounds. They could save time when going on a journey, for they no longer had to walk miles along the river bank to find a shallow place where they could wade across. They could trade and exchange things with tribes who lived on the other side. More and more bridges were built.

As years went by, men got better at making bridges. They learnt how to fasten many pieces of wood together. They learnt how to cut pieces of stone and shape them so that they fitted together like building bricks. They built bridges long enough to cross wide rivers. They built bridges wide enough so that several men could cross at once, or even a horse and cart. They built sides, called *parapets*, so that no one would fall off.

The Romans, who were good at many things, were especially good at building bridges. They would place piles of flat stones in the river. These were called *piers*. Then they would use lengths of wood to stretch across as spans. But their best bridges were made entirely of stones. Sometimes, the stones were joined together by mortar, made by mixing lime and sand. At other times, the stones were cut so carefully that they fitted together like the pieces of a jigsaw puzzle and needed no mortar.

Some Roman bridges were very fine indeed and the stones were arranged to make round arches. In the South of France there is a wonderful Roman bridge called the Pont du Gard, a bridge made to carry water as well as traffic. A 'water' bridge is called an *aqueduct*. You can still walk across this one, two thousand years after it was built, or drive a car across the lower part, for it is really two bridges in one.

One of the most famous bridges in England was Old London Bridge. It was made of stone and had nineteen arches. It had houses built all along it. They were narrow but quite tall. Some even had little gardens and a cellar. At one end of the bridge was a church, so that travellers could say their prayers before going on a journey. There were shops, too, and a drawbridge at one end so that it could be closed. Old London Bridge stood for six hundred years before it was knocked down to make way for a new bridge.

In 1778, the first iron bridge was made in England. It was placed over the River Severn at Coalbrookdale, in Shropshire. It was made in pieces which were bolted together. Everyone thought it was a very fine bridge, so fine that when a town grew up round it they called the town Ironbridge. Bridge and town are still there.

Even larger bridges were built and men were able to cross wide stretches of water. One of the biggest of the new bridges was the Menai Suspension Bridge. It joined the island of Anglesey to the mainland of Wales. It was called a *suspension* bridge because the roadway was suspended, or held, by giant chains. It was a great success.

Steel and concrete began to be used in bridge building. Steel is much stronger than iron. A famous steel bridge is the one which carries the railway across the Firth of Forth in Scotland. Here huge frames of steel are balanced on island piers, their criss-cross arms stretching out on either side until they join the next arms. This kind of bridge is known as a *cantilever* bridge. It is two kilometres long. Not long ago, another bridge was built over the Forth quite near the old one. This new one is a suspension bridge, one of the largest in the world. It carries the road.

In Washington State, U.S.A., there is a new bridge which *floats* on the river. The floating part is two kilometres long. But perhaps the most famous bridge in the world is the Sydney Harbour Bridge in Australia. A great steel arch carries four railway tracks, a wide road and two footpaths.

A very odd thing happened to the Tacoma Bridge in

America. It was built in 1940 and was a suspension bridge. Soon after it was finished, people noticed that it swayed from side to side and tilted when the wind blew. Worse still, the roadway on the bridge used to rise up and down, in hills and valleys, when strong winds blew. People called the Tacoma Bridge 'Galloping Gertie'. But four months after it opened, part of it broke away and it all had to be rebuilt. Now it no longer 'gallops'.

Soon, no doubt, newer and even better ways of building bridges will be discovered. How surprised the caveman with the tree trunk would be if he could see modern bridges!

Greyman

In a lonely part of Iceland there lived, many years ago, a man and his wife. They rented their cottage from the local Baron and had a cow, a few pots and pans and not much more. One Sunday the man went to church, but instead of dropping off to sleep during the sermon, as he usually did, he listened to the parson preaching.

The parson said that all men should be generous and be ready to give away some of the things they owned. Whatever they gave, he said, they would get back a thousand times. This interested the man from the cottage and he went home and told his wife about it.

"The parson says that whatever we give away we will get back a thousandfold," he told his wife.

"I don't believe it," sniffed the wife. "I expect you only heard part of what he said. You know you always drop off to sleep during the sermon."

But the husband stuck to his story. A thousandfold the parson had said, and a thousandfold he had meant. Husband and wife argued about it for the rest of the evening.

The next day the man went out and pulled down his cow-shed and started making arrangements to build one large enough for a thousand cows. His neighbours (and his wife) thought he was crazy. Didn't he understand the troubles that owning a thousand cows could bring? But the man would have none of it and began thinking to whom he should give his cow, so that he could have a thousand cows in return. The first person he thought of was the parson himself, so he tied a rope round the cow's neck and went off with it to see the parson.

The parson was quite surprised when he opened the front door and saw a man waiting there with a cow.

"What's all this?" he asked angrily, for the cow's back legs were in the flower bed.

"I've brought this cow for you," said the man, and he reminded the parson of his sermon.

The parson was very cross indeed. He said that was not what he meant. He was very rude and sent the man and his cow away with a torrent of words round their ears which were quite unsuitable for a parson.

The man was downcast and the cow wasn't very pleased either, as a cold wind had got up from the north. Then it began to snow, and when it snows in Iceland it really does snow. Before long the man had lost his way. Man and cow were almost disappearing in the snow-drifts when a large person with a frozen beard came into sight. He was carrying a huge bag on his back.

"Whatever are you doing out with a cow in this weather?" enquired the bearded stranger, his beard making cracking noises as he spoke. He listened to the whole story of the sermon, and the torn-down cow-shed and the disgruntled parson.

"It seems to me," said the icy stranger, "that you would be better off with this bag I am carrying. With it you have a good chance of getting home. Let us exchange."

"What's in the bag?" asked our man.

"Flesh and bones," answered the bearded one. So they struck a bargain and the stranger went off with the cow and our man started to drag the bag, for it was remarkably heavy. Then, to his surprise, he found he was almost standing on his doorstep.

The wife was delighted to see her husband safely home, of course, but when he told her he had exchanged the cow for a bag of flesh and bones she flew into a mighty rage. When she had finished saying lots of things, all meaning roughly that her husband was an idiot, she fetched her largest pot, filled it with water and said, "Well, we may as well have some soup from this bag of flesh and bones. We have little else to eat."

When the water began to boil the husband untied the bag and out leaped a young man dressed from head to heel in grey.

"I would make terrible soup," he said.

The husband was speechless with surprise, but his wife wasn't. She said lots of things, mostly about her stupid husband. He had lost their cow, so there was no milk, and he had brought home another mouth to feed. She threw a few saucepans and a frying-pan at her husband.

The Greyman listened to them quarrelling for a time and then he said, "Let me go out and see if I can find something for us to eat. You won't gain anything at all by quarrelling."

So off he went into the night, and in a very short time indeed he was back carrying the carcass of a sheep.

"Here you are," he said, "pop this into the pot."

And so the Greyman (he never said what his real name

was) settled in with the man and his wife. He worked about the place and made himself useful, and whenever food was a little short he always managed to turn up with something or other, usually the carcass of a sheep. The man and wife didn't think to ask where he got the meat.

Now the local Baron's shepherd began to be puzzled. Something was wrong. He was sure that the flock of sheep he looked after was dwindling. He found it very difficult to count his sheep because counting sheep always made him drop off to sleep. At last he went to his master and told him of his suspicions.

"H'm," said the Baron. "None of my neighbours would steal from me. They would not dare. It must be someone else. Are there any strangers about?"

He was told about the Greyman who had been seen pottering about the neighbourhood.

"Bring him to me," ordered the Baron.

When the Greyman was brought before him, the Baron said, "Many of my sheep are missing. I think they have been stolen. Do you know anything about them?"

"Indeed I do," answered the Greyman calmly. "I took them." The Baron nearly fell off his chair with surprise.

"Why did you do this thing?" he spluttered.

"I took the sheep," said the Greyman, "because the couple I live with are poor and have little to eat, while you, Sire, have more than enough which is not being used. It seems to me fairer that they should have a little of what you don't need, rather than they should starve while you have too much."

The Baron was flabbergasted. He had never met a rascal like this one. He asked the Greyman if stealing was the only thing he was good at, or was it the thing he liked doing best, or was it just a hobby.

The Greyman only smiled sweetly.

The Baron found himself curiously charmed by the young man. He ought to know more about him.

"You know," he said at last, "you deserve to be hanged for this crime, but I will pardon you if you can prove you are as skilled as you seem to be. I shall send my prize bull to graze in the forest tomorrow with six men in attendance. If you can steal it from them you will be forgiven. But if you fail you shall die."

"Steal a bull from six guards!" exclaimed the Greyman, "That's almost impossible!"

"Maybe it is impossible," said the Baron, "but that's your problem."

The Greyman went back to the cottage. The man and wife were glad to see him for they had thought he would never return from the Baron's court. The Greyman told them that he had to steal the prize bull guarded by six men if he wished to live.

Next morning he went off into the forest to a place which he knew the Baron's men would need to pass in order to get the bull to the grazing patch. He climbed a tree by the path, and with a length of rope he had brought with him, he made it look as if he had hanged himself.

A short time later, along came the six men with the prize bull. When they caught sight of the Greyman apparently hanging lifeless from a tree, they were quite pleased. They thought he had been up to his thieving tricks elsewhere and had been hanged by someone else. So, being a lazy lot, they thought they need not bother about being watchful and they went on their way fooling about.

No sooner were they out of sight than the Greyman climbed down and ran silently through the forest by another path until he was in front of them again. He climbed a tree and did his hanging act again.

Shortly afterwards, the six men with the bull appeared. They looked up and saw the Greyman hanging there. They scratched their heads. They were very puzzled and, perhaps, a little frightened.

"There must be two of 'em," grunted one of the guards.

"I don't like the look of it," said one.

"This is a rum do!" observed another.

"Let's go back and check," suggested yet another. But none was willing to be left alone in the forest, and the bull got bad-tempered if he was pulled about too much. They decided to tie the bull to a tree and all go back to the spot where they had first seen the Greyman hanging.

The moment they were out of sight again the Greyman slipped down the tree, untied the bull and made for the cottage at top speed. The couple were terrified when they saw the bull tied to their fence. Anyway, they didn't want the fence pulled down. As for the guards, they soon found out that they had been tricked and hurried to the Baron to break the news of the Greyman's success.

Again the Baron sent for the Greyman.

"Did you steal my bull?" he asked.

"I did, Sire," answered the Greyman, "I had to, to save my life." The Baron was getting impatient and wanted the Greyman out of the way, but because he was a Baron he had to appear just and fair.

"Very well," he said, "but you must undertake one more task if your life is to be spared."

"And what's that?" asked the Greyman.

"You must steal both me and my wife out of our bed."

"That cannot be done," said the Greyman.

"Maybe not," answered the Baron, "but that's how it is. You must succeed if you wish to live." And he dismissed the Greyman from the court.

The Greyman went back to the cottage and borrowed an old top hat which had been lying about for years, because top hats are not popular in Iceland. In the top hat he cut holes into which he fixed candles. He borrowed a couple of sacks as well, and late that night off he went to the church, which was opposite the Baron's house. When he got to the church he went into the tower and set all the bells jangling. Then he lit the candles in his hat and stood near the church door.

The Baron and his wife, hearing the bells in the middle of the night, wondered what on earth the parson was doing and, leaving their bed, went to the window to see what all the din was about. They saw near the church door the shape of a man from whom beams of light shone forth. They thought it must be an angel from heaven come down to earth with good tidings. They hastened to dress in their best clothes and jewels and rushed across to the church. Keeping their heads bowed, they knelt before the figure of light which they took to be an angel and begged that all their sins might be forgiven. The 'angel' replied that all their sins would be forgiven but first, as a punishment, they must spend a short time in the two sacks he held. This struck the Baron and his wife as a peculiar but easy price to pay for forgiveness, and in they crawled. The 'angel' tied the bags tightly with them inside.

Unfortunately, the bags had previously held something with an unpleasant smell. The Baron and his wife were soon thumping about, begging to be released.

The Greyman then told them that he was no angel. He was the young man who had taken the Baron's sheep, captured his prize bull and now, as the Baron had asked him to, stolen him and his wife from their bed. If he was given a solemn promise that he would be asked to perform no more tasks, and that the couple would live rent free in the cottage for the rest of their lives, then he would release them.

The Baron saw there was nothing for it but to agree. The Greyman untied the sacks and disappeared. No one knows where. But the Baron thought it wise to keep his promise and the couple lived in comfort for the rest of their lives. So, in a way, the husband who gave away his cow received its value back a thousandfold, which was what the parson had said in his sermon.

Checkpoint 

How well did you read?

What did the husband usually do in church?

Why was the parson angry when the husband called on him?

What did the icy stranger say there was in the bag?

Why did the shepherd have trouble in counting his sheep?

What did Greyman do to the top hat?

What happened to Greyman in the end?

Choose

Here are four words from the story:

flabbergasted
solemn
downcast
disgruntled

Which would you choose for these pictures?